DISCIPLINE
FOR HOME AND SCHOOL

BOOK TWO

Books by Edward E. Ford:

Discipline for Home and School, Book Two: Practical Standards for Schools, Revised and Expanded *

Discipline for Home and School, Book One, Revised and Expanded *

Freedom from Stress *

Love Guaranteed: A Better Marriage in Eight Weeks *

Choosing to Love: A New Way to Respond *

Permanent Love: Practical Steps to a Lasting Relationship (with Steven L. Englund) *

Why Marriage?

Why Be Lonely? (with Robert L. Zorn)

For the Love of Children (with Steven L. Englund)

Money Isn't Enough (with Jim Soldani)

Chapters by the author in:

What Are You Doing? How People Are Helped Through Reality Therapy. Naomi Glasser, editor. Harper & Row, 1980.

Family Counseling and Therapy. Arthur M. Horne and Merle M. Ohlsen, editors. F. E. Peacock, 1982.

Volitional Action. Wayne Hershberger, editor. North-Holland, 1989.

* Available from: Brandt Publishing, 10209 N. 56th Street, Scottsdale, AZ 85253, phone 480-991-4860

DISCIPLINE
FOR HOME AND SCHOOL

BOOK TWO
PRACTICAL STANDARDS FOR SCHOOLS

REVISED AND EXPANDED EDITION

EDWARD E. FORD

Foreword by W. Thomas Bourbon, Ph.D.

Introduction by Joseph Sierzenga

Brandt Publishing

Design & Typesetting: Greg Williams, Gravel Switch, KY
Printing & Packaging: O'Neil Printing, Phoenix, AZ

Library of Congress Catalog Card Number: 99-072087

ISBN 0-9616716-8-8

Printed in the United States of America

5   4   3   2   1

Brandt Publishing
10209 North 56th Street
Scottsdale, AZ 85253
480-991-4860

Contents

Drawings by Margaret Carey, Brisbane, Australia

To George Venetis
and
LeEdna Custer-Knight

without their belief in me and dedication,
this program would never have become a reality

And to my brother Tom
who died in November 1998
and
his wife Susan

their encouragement and support for RTP
have helped me build the needed integrity
into this project that will open the possibility
for millions of children to find, through RTP,
the respect, the self-confidence, and
the self-discipline they so desperately need

Acknowledgements

What have been most rewarding about the development of this program are the close friendships I've made. In writing this book, George Venetis, assistant principal at Clarendon and Solano, was extremely helpful. His 28 years in education, including eight as an administrator, and especially his skills and his insights into the workings of a school, have been invaluable. The dedication he's given to my program is overwhelming. George is not only a great educator, filled with integrity, but a close friend, for which I'm very appreciative.

Another close friend is Tom Bourbon, who taught psychology for more than 25 years in a university and did research on the brain in neurological departments of medical universities. Presently he is independently researching perceptual control theory. Tom has spent the past four years visiting and working with me in schools here in the United States, in Australia, and in Singapore. He has been supported by a grant to study the Responsible Thinking Process (RTP), and his insights and suggestions have been critical in the development of RTP. Without Tom, the process would be far less effective than it is now.

The work and support of LeEdna Custer-Knight, Clarendon school psychologist, has been overwhelming. Her work with and dedication to children, especially the seriously disadvantaged, provide an example for all educators. I've known her to spend hours of her own time dealing with children who no longer attend Clarendon. LeEdna has become a close friend and source of inspiration. She is one of the best examples I know of a truly dedicated educator.

Darleen Martin continues as responsible thinking classroom teacher at Clarendon. Her gentle but firm way of dealing with children helped mold my conception of the ideal
RTC teacher. Her dedication to this process, to the concepts, and her willingness to spend hours with those from
other schools, even when overwhelmed in her own job,
make her another example of a dedicated educator.

I've made three trips to Australia. They've been exhila-
rating and inspirational because of Tim Carey. His ability to
think things through and then to ask demanding questions
has forced me to re-examine much of what I do. For example, his continual insistence that I include more of PCT in
RTP training has been critical in helping educators understand the importance of maintaining the integrity of the
process. Tim and his wife, Margaret, have really defined and
solidified the intervention team concept in Chapter 14. A
special thanks to Margaret for her delightful drawings,
which are fine additions to both *Book One* and this book.

I'm most appreciative of another close friend, Joe Sierzenga. Sadly, Joe died in September 1997 after being struck
by another car while driving to school. I wrote a memorial
to Joe at the beginning of the revised edition of *Discipline
for Home and School, Book One*. Joe and I had worked
closely from the very beginning on the development of RTP,
especially in relation to perceptual control theory. Joe,
along with George, LeEdna, Tom, Darleen, and Tim, are the
core group of educators who have been helping me in the
formation and evolution of RTP.

There are many others. Some have written or contributed in various ways to chapters. Others have made comments on the back covers of this book or *Book One*. I am
sincerely appreciative to all of these dedicated educators.

A special thanks to Greg Williams, who did the final edit-
ing and typesetting. I always feel relieved when everything
is in Greg's hands. I know it will come out right.

Ed Ford
Phoenix, Arizona

Foreword

Edward Ford was trained as a social worker, and I as a laboratory research psychologist. In the usual order of things, people from our backgrounds might not meet. How is it, then, that I am writing the Foreword to Ed Ford's second book about discipline? In 1982, I organized the first meeting of people interested in perceptual control theory (PCT), which was originated by William T. Powers. Ed Ford was one of the seven people who attended, and he has attended many subsequent meetings of the Control Systems Group. Ed was not trained as a scientist, but for as long as I have known him, he has worked diligently to understand the scientific basis of PCT and the phenomenon it explains: people behave to control their own perceptions, their own experiences of the world. We have spent many hours, over many years, talking about PCT science. In his *Discipline for Home and School, Book One*, Ed described his Responsible Thinking Process (RTP). Ed tried to ground RTP in PCT science. When some of his colleagues from the public schools joined Ed at our meetings and described dramatic positive results using RTP, some of us who do laboratory research on PCT wondered if it could be as good as they said. Then I went to Phoenix to visit several schools that used RTP. I went with three major questions in mind: (1) Does RTP produce dramatic positive changes in schools? (2) If it does that, does RTP have anything at all to do with PCT science and the fact that people behave to control their own experiences? (3) Is RTP just and fair, in the PCT sense of those words—does it help students who have disrupted in school learn to become better at controlling their own experiences, without unnecessarily disrupting other people while they control theirs?

What I saw on that first visit convinced me that some of the dramatic accounts of RTP were correct, but I also saw schools where it did not work all that well. We wondered why the results could be so different. A few months later, I obtained a grant through Philanthropic Ventures Foundation in California to study that issue for a year, while I visited more schools where RTP was used. After visiting dozens of schools, we have a clear picture of why RTP works extremely well in some schools, less well in some others, and very poorly in a few. In this book, Ed and others describe practical standards that can help a school achieve success with RTP. I believe these standards are different from those you will see for most other discipline processes—if they even have standards. You see, the standards are not made up by Ed; they are descriptions of what people do in the schools where RTP works best. This book shows that RTP is not about something you do to students to make them behave, once and for all. Instead, it is a continuing process, built on mutual respect, that can make a profound difference, but only if people work diligently to help children, not to control them. RTP works best when the educators understand that children and educators alike behave to control their own experiences. When RTP works best, children understand that, too.

W. Thomas Bourbon, Ph.D.
Rochelle, Texas

Introduction

We begin to learn about discipline as a student in kindergarten. From these experiences, we each develop an individual way of thinking about how students behave. From our experiences in school as well as how we are dealt with at home, we set standards that reflect the way children should behave in school. If we choose to go into education, we make our decisions on how we treat our students based on our past experiences and the standards they reflect.

Much of what we do in the area of student discipline has its origins in these experiences, which then become the foundation for how we will deal with our own students. And whether we think seriously about it or not, our approach is based upon some psychological theory. Research has found that many educators are unable to cite the specific theory of behavior upon which many of their decisions are made.

In his book *Discipline for Home and School*, Ed developed a systems approach to student discipline, which he calls the Responsible Thinking Process. This comprehensive approach demands an entirely new way of looking at what students do and how they think. Ed has gone beyond suggesting general observations that appear to be effective in a school setting, a trend that fills most discipline programs today. He's not afraid to work with teachers and administrators in the classroom, demonstrating his ideas and techniques. And what he teaches has made a significant difference in the climate of schools.

First, he challenges us to learn and apply perceptual control theory as the psychological base for handling student disruptions and assisting students in the Responsible Thinking Process. Although the theory seems much like others, it will revolutionize the way people interact with each other. The proof is in what is happening in the schools that have successfully applied his program. Unlike most programs, it works—and not just in pleasant suburban settings, but in very tough inner-city schools, from elementary through high school, including correctional and boarding schools.

Discipline for Home and School, Book Two takes Ed's program to a new level. After Ed and Tom Bourbon, a behavioral research scientist, evaluated over 30 school districts nationally that have implemented this program, they began to see standards that successful programs had in common. These standards of effectiveness reflect Ed's systems approach to student discipline and responsible thinking, and they will help any educator consider the implementation of this program. These program standards will enable individual members of the school organization to achieve individual goals, as well as the goals of the organization. They are the bridge between the systems of ideas described in *Discipline for Home and School* and the decisions we make on an individual daily basis.

School districts that are willing to give up control of certain individual perceptions of student behavior and motivation will find this program to be the most exciting and rewarding initiative they have ever undertaken.

Ed has outlined the necessary standards for implementing a successful discipline program as they apply to politics, commitment, roles, and unexpected developments. As an elementary administrator and chairperson of our Discipline Strategic Planning Committee for the Morrice Area School District, it is clear to me that these program standards will force us to decide whether we want to continue to build a model program or not. After committing to the program, adoption of these program standards, which reflect the integrity of the process and have a proven track record, will enhance the success rate of the program. By clearly defining what is expected at the different levels of the school organization, each member has the opportunity to align individual goals with the goals of the organization. This will reduce conflict within the system as we control our individual perceptions along with the goals of the organization.

This is the most powerful and innovative approach to student discipline and student responsibility I have experienced in the past 18 years. Ed has taken his program through the three levels of research that qualify it in our district as "best knowledge" and as eligible for board adoption and implementation.

At level I, he researched perceptual control theory and developed practical applications for the school setting. Ed then built a program model at the Clarendon Elementary School in the Osborn School District in Phoenix to test the validity of his process, level II. At level III, Ed put more than 30 of the schools that were implementing his program nationally through a critical on-site evaluation. This program is the only one that does continual and critical analysis of itself to certify the quality of the process and the integrity of the model.

I have found these program standards to be the components necessary to elevate our school discipline program from an implementing school to a model program.

Joseph Sierzenga
Former Principal
Morrice Elementary School
Morrice, Michigan
1996

Part 1. How to Make RTP Work Well

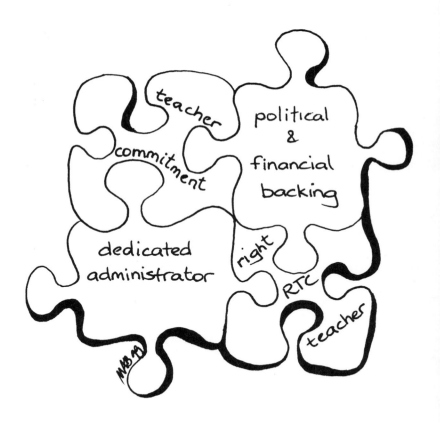

Chapter 1
Four Keys to Success

In January 1994, my Responsible Thinking Process (RTP) was created at the Clarendon Elementary School in the Osborn School District in Phoenix. Since then, it has spread to more than 150 schools throughout the U.S. and more than 50 in Australia, and to Singapore, Germany, and other countries as well. The participating schools service children of all ages, from special education preschool through primary to high school. Their locations range from the inner city to suburban and rural settings, including boarding schools on the Navajo reservation and a juvenile lockup facility in Tucson.

As I've worked with these schools, the elements needed to create a Responsible Thinking Process became apparent. Usually a committed few read my discipline book, view the TV news video, review the process, and then recommend to their staff and peers that RTP is worth considering for adoption. If the teachers and staff agree, books are purchased for everyone. If there is a consensus to move forward, then a day or two of training is scheduled for the entire staff. If there is still a strong commitment from both the administration and a large majority of teachers, the process is implemented and does well. Unfortunately, in some schools where staff members follow the same pattern of learning about the process, RTP does not do well. For example, I visited one school several months after extensive training, with a highly committed principal, and found an unskilled parent in charge of the responsible thinking classroom (RTC). For the half hour I was in that classroom, not once was the process used. The students talked, taunted the parent, and played games as they moved about the room. In short, the place was in total chaos.

In every successful school, there are *four critical goals that must be established and maintained*. Otherwise, the money spent will be wasted, the teachers and staff will be frustrated, and parents will see their children once again be cheated of a full-time education. These four goals are: 1) the necessary political and financial backing, 2) teacher commitment, 3) the right RTC teacher in the right RTC, and 4) a dedicated administrator. If these requirements are not in place, there will be increasing classroom disruption, which will rob students of the education they so desperately need and will discourage teachers and administrators from remaining in education. Many of those who remain either are in denial that the problem exists or continue to blame others for their discipline problems.

Please note: Before you continue reading this book, it is very important that you have read Discipline for Home and School, Book One, *which presents the basic ideas underlying RTP.*

In order to protect the integrity of the process, Responsible Thinking Process, Inc. is offering recognition to those schools that are successful in the use of RTP. This recognition, in the form of certification, is given when the administrator and responsible thinking classroom teacher are both performing their roles, all of the teachers, with very few exceptions, are using the process, and appropriate data have been kept for one year. Only educators who have been recommended by RTP, Inc. as trainers should be used by schools wishing to learn the process.

Chapter 2
Getting Your Financial
and Political Ducks in Order

I remember one school administrator who asked me to present my ideas. As I spoke to his staff in this urban school, I felt an intense interest and an eager desire to understand the process. As at any presentation, I had brought along a few copies of *Discipline for Home and School, Book One*, in case anyone wanted to read more about the Responsible Thinking Process. At the end of my presentation, all 30 discipline books were purchased. The desire for help and to understand the process was overwhelming. Later I learned that the superintendent, the assistant, and the school board refused to allow the school staff to proceed further with the implementation of RTP. Without the approval and commitment to the process or financial support by the school board and district office, any venture by an individual school is tenuous.

I was fortunate with my model process. The initial support for the process at Clarendon and Solano came from the parent organizations. The decision to enlist the support of the PTA and later the teacher's association's own financial commitment helped to fund the training for the process and to drive the process through various administrative hurdles, especially since both Clarendon and Solano were site-based driven.

After political support is forthcoming, funding becomes the central problem. I recently worked in one district where cutbacks allowed for only a very inexperienced aide for the responsible thinking classroom (RTC). Without an experienced professional, the process has only a slight chance of success. An experienced teacher in the RTC is more likely to be able to detect special education needs, then refer the child for testing. Also, classroom teachers are more likely to respect the decisions of the supervisor of the RTC if that person is a qualified teacher. Schools have found parents are more accepting of the process when they learn their child is with a teacher, a college-trained professional who is ready to help when their child wants help creating a plan to resolve her problems or needs help on a homework assignment, while waiting to return to class and negotiate with the teacher.

However, many schools, because of lack of funds, simply cannot afford a professional teacher. Instead, they have turned to the many nonprofessionals who work in schools or to parents active in the PTO who are attracted to the job. Most of these nonprofessionals have done an exceptional job in the RTC. I've found them to be totally committed. They work hard to develop the skills required of the RTC teacher. After only a few months, they have earned the respect and admiration of the rest of the staff, especially administrators and certified teachers. It is not unusual to find on their desks well-used copies of my discipline books.

Many administrators oppose RTP on the grounds that it is too expensive. What most who argue against the added cost of RTP forget is that there is a tremendous increase in instruction time in all of the classrooms. In the various schools that have shown an interest in RTP, mostly in inner-city settings, when I first give a presentation on the process, I've asked teachers what percentage of their teaching time has been taken up with discipline or classroom management. With rare exceptions, I've been told anywhere from 30% to as high as 85% of classroom time has been spent on disruption. Pauline Rudloff and Paul Pegany, both sixth grade teachers at Clarendon, told me that, prior to RTP, 85% of their time was spent on discipline, versus less than 10% now. The same is true for Sharon Pegany, a fourth grade teacher at Clarendon.

Most teachers are highly competent educators. Since they are expected to deal with disruptive children, they are highly frustrated at not being able to teach where the disruptions are usually very few. Also, those children wanting to learn are being robbed of valuable instruction time. A key test of any discipline process is whether it increases the instructional time of the teacher and improves the climate for learning. Another test is whether there is a growing mutual respect between the chronic acting-out children and the teachers and staff. Finally, there is the question of whether all of the students are following school rules *by learning to think through and then implement successful ways of handling problems*. This, with the help of teachers, can only be done through efficient plan making.

Actually, I've found that once the teachers experience relief from the tension of constant discipline problems, resulting in a doubling—and sometimes tripling—of class teaching time, they are more than willing to accept an increase in class size, rather than lose RTP. Obviously, not all gains are this great, especially in most suburban settings. Most of my experience lies with urban populations. Which brings me to the second key to assuring the success of the process: teacher commitment.

Chapter 3
Teachers Must Be Totally Committed to Changing How They Deal with Students

This process demands an entirely new way of perceiving children and how they think. Often teachers and administrators fail to realize they are actually teaching their students to reorganize how they think when faced with conflicting goals. *This requires a whole new way of working with children*, which, for a few teachers, is hard to accept. For many teachers, it is not hard to learn and accept, but others, including many who've learned and used the process successfully, slip back easily into old habitual ways of telling and yelling at students. And some teachers, who are having difficulty dealing with responsibility in their own lives, find teaching these life skills to children a little overwhelming. (See teacher's letter at the end of this chapter.)

Without continual support and a thorough understanding of the process by the faculty, the process will fail. I know a principal who was really sold on the effectiveness of RTP, and yet the faculty voted overwhelmingly against it. I was asked by the superintendent of one district to present RTP to his administration and faculty, who showed no interest. Teacher buy-in is critical. I also find it wiser to begin with one building in a district and develop a model. Once successful, it can serve as an example for the rest of the schools.

When reacting to an event, most children deal with whatever gets in the way of their reaching a goal. RTP distracts them from their original goal, which is to control their own experiences. It centers the students on their actions, which are the means by which they control their own experiences. Our minds are always focused on what we are trying to control: our perceptions. The first RTP question gets us to look at the means by which we are controlling our perceptions, which is how we behave. Thus, "What are you doing?" attempts to get children to focus on their present behavior or way of acting. Then, the RTP question that follows ("What are the rules?") attempts to get them to tie their behavior to the disturbance that they are causing to others, for which rules act as a guide. Often, there are unintended consequences when we act. We leave the front door open on a cold and windy day, or we leave a towel on the bathroom floor or food on the kitchen table. Often, we are unaware of these actions. After all, the purpose of any rule is to act as a guide or standard, so that as we attempt to satisfy our own goals or desires, we don't infringe on the rights of others who are trying to satisfy their own goals. This is why I insist that the critical rule in both home and school should be "you cannot violate the rights of others." Most teachers report that after they've used the RTP questions for a while, their students learn to make the connection between what they are doing and whether what they are doing is disturbing others. They have learned to think this through. They immediately compare what they are doing with whether they are "breaking the rules" and thus keeping others from what they are trying to do. Now the children think this way wherever they go.

The additional questions "lead" children through an organized way of thinking by asking them to look at the down-the-road consequences of their own actions as they relate to the rules. The third question is "What happens when you break the rules?" That is followed by "Is that what you want to happen to you?" Actually, what the teachers and administrators are doing is helping children to transform the way they think, to develop the habit of first looking at their actions as they relate to the local rules (and perhaps their own rules) before deciding on a course of action that will help them get what they want. If the local school board requires the district's administrators to respect the local rules and customs of the community they serve, then the issue of cross-cultural concerns is respected.

It usually takes a while for most children to develop this pattern of thought, to transform the way they think. And it often takes longer for the school staff to develop the habit of continually asking these types of questions.

In a number of schools where I've worked, a common problem with the school staff, especially teachers and administrators, is that they have been held accountable for years for controlling student behavior. They are rewarded for being effective at "controlling" their students, and they are censured for those students who they have sent to the office from their classrooms or who have created problems for the district office. Many student problems have been masked in the classroom by teachers not wanting to be perceived as "inadequate" due to their apparent inability to deal effectively with students within the classroom setting. With the use of RTP, there is a major shift in how teachers are perceived by others and by themselves.

Teachers who've felt they "didn't have any problems," and were perceived by others as not having problems, hated to admit that they did indeed have problems. This imagined ability to "control" students was part of their teaching administrative ability, and they were reluctant to open themselves to any kind of perceived change. But in reality, everyone knows how well everyone else is doing. RTP demands honesty not only with the students, but also among those in the faculty. And, more importantly, within one's self. This shifting of accountability, according to many teachers, is what relieves the stress, because now responsibility for one's own actions is rightly assigned to where it should be. Namely, students and staff alike are responsible each for their own individual behaviors.

The critical issue for everyone is to allow time to get used to the new process. According to one RTC teacher in an urban high school, half of the teachers brought into the process began using it right away. In two to four weeks, another 40% of the teachers slowly began to use the process. It was hard for some teachers to allow the first student to make the choice to leave their room. They still believed they would be held accountable for the referrals; that sense of accountability hadn't totally gone away. They had been told it was OK to let students choose to leave the classroom, and that no administrative judgment would be forthcoming. But some habits are hard to break, and beliefs are hard to change. It took a while for teachers to get used to the idea that when students leave the classroom, the students, not the teachers, are held accountable.

Some teachers wanted to test the program and see what happened to a student. They allowed one student to choose to leave the room and report to the RTC. Once teachers sensed that they weren't being held accountable for the disruptive student and saw that the process really did work, they became more relaxed and accepting of the process. That's why it's so important for support to come from the teachers. Their input on the initial exposure to RTP is critical to its successful adoption.

As I said in *Book One*, most adults tell children what to do. When you tell children what to do, you are teaching them to depend on you, not to think for themselves. If what they are told conflicts with their own goals, they tend to perceive the staff and the institution as a roadblock or barrier, as a disturbance to their system. What follows is their reluctance to work within the system, and they tend to fight the system and everyone in it. What is worse, they never learn to think through all of the steps that RTP teaches.

When they are confronted by adults who tell them everything they must do, many children give up, especially when they are told different things in different settings. They learn to become dependent on what others tell them. The best analogy is the classic case of an inmate released from prison after 30 or 40 years. He has long since lost the sense of how to adjust and deal with the strange new culture that confronts him. To a lesser degree, the same can be true with children. I've done numerous group meetings in juvenile correctional facilities. In one such group, several of the teenagers complained about the lack of problem solving and critical thinking in the school curriculum. As one juvenile put it, "They're teaching us math and history. Man, I don't know how to get a job, how to get along with a girl, how to make it on the outside. Most of us are scared when we get out. They want us to go straight, and all we know is selling stuff."

They've been told specifically what not to do, or else face the consequences. Somehow, the consequences are supposed to magically teach them how to become responsible and deal effectively with their lives. And juveniles are told not only what to do, but when to do it, how to do it, and where to do it. But is that kind of dependency going to help them when they get out of lockup? What really does help children create harmony in their own lives? It has to be their ability to think through the various problems they face. Does telling or yelling or punishing or rewarding children teach them how to think on their own? The treatment or lockup facility helps juveniles develop the habit of "doing what they're told." Complying with direct orders has become the most hassle-free route for the juvenile.

When juveniles do not learn to think for themselves, they get caught up in their old ways of functioning. *They've become institutionalized*, like the long-term convict who has been locked up for many years. If children don't learn to think, they'll react to satisfy immediate goals without reflecting on possible consequences. Those around them are considered as disturbances to their goals, and the juveniles are going to fight them. But more often, they learn to go along to get along. This tell and yell way of dealing with children is not limited to correctional or residential settings. It also occurs in schools and homes. When children are asked questions in a calm, curious, respectful way, they tend to calm down. They become more open to learning how to think through their difficulties. In this atmosphere, institutionalization becomes a thing of the past. Instead, students learn to think, and they deal with their problems in a responsible way, by making effective plans and negotiating with the teacher. Thus, the teacher is no longer perceived as a disturbance. Instead, many students will see the teacher as someone *who is interested in their world and respects what they have to say in a non-critical way. In this climate, mutual respect has the best chance of growing.* Yelling and telling just creates chaos and dependency. Rewarding creates dependency on rewards and requires that the child find some importance to the rewards. In fact, rewarding can be very demeaning. Try giving your spouse, or someone with whom you are close, some money when they've shown you a kindness. One thing rewarding does *not* do is teach children to think.

The principal of an urban high school in Phoenix came up with some interesting student reactions to RTP. Several of his administrators, in talking with the students, found that their criticism had nothing to do with the process or the responsible thinking classroom, but was that "some of the teachers aren't using the questions." It seems that they preferred being shown respect through the questioning process to having teachers order them around or tell them what they were doing wrong.

Thus, asking in a respectful way creates mutual respect. If teachers stop using the questions, chaos and conflict will return. That is why it is so important for teachers to commit to continually using this process, not only in the classroom, but wherever they are in the school environment. This leads to the third key factor: the responsible thinking teacher and the responsible thinking classroom. But first, consider the following letter written by a member of the staff of Clarendon Elementary School (reprinted here with permission). LeEdna Custer-Knight is the school psychologist at Clarendon.

November 22, 1994

LeEdna, & Ed Ford,

   I want to thank you for the staff meeting of November 21. I really needed the encouragement of staying on task with the responsibility thinking program that you have worked so hard to institute here. I believe in this program, but I must confess I had also become sloppy in keeping with the program. An occasional meeting would probably be good for all of us.

There has been something I've always wanted to say about this program, but never had the courage. The questions I'm required to ask students who are making poor choices are difficult for me because I, too, do not take responsibility for my actions. I have spent a life time blaming what I do on other people rather than realizing that I, and I alone, chose to do or say certain things. While others' actions and words certainly affect my thinking, I have had to learn and accept responsibility for my own decisions and actions and the consequences of those. It was challenging, to say the least, to teach a life principle that I have not yet learned. I'm working on it. I guess what I'm saying to you two is that this program has helped me a lot in my own personal life. The reason it takes courage to share this is this whole thing is a gentle reminder to me that so much of my life would be different had I known how to make responsible decisions. Even though I really haven't told you anything about myself, I feel as though I am sharing a very private part of me. Even today, so many of the struggles that I have could be resolved by responsible thinking. (I have taken a form home and am working on it!) As I read back over this paragraph, I realize that anyone who is honest with themselves could have written this!!

Thanks again. You have both been great. Even though I don't work closely with you two, I see the results of your work in our students. I greatly admire and respect your work. How I wish I had someone like you when I was a child.

Chapter 4
The Right Responsible Thinking
Teacher in the Right Classroom Setting

I've worked in a number of schools where the process is highly successful. In those schools, it is obvious that the right RTC teacher is needed in the right setting. Darleen Martin, RTC teacher at Clarendon, who helped me develop this process when I first began to work at Clarendon, is a shining example of the right person in the right place. Her calm but firm approach plus her dedication made creating the process much easier.

I'm constantly impressed with the number of creative ideas that come from the various responsible thinking classrooms. Darleen still continues to look for ways to improve the process, especially as it pertains to her RTC. At the beginning of each year, she invites all classes to tour the responsible thinking classroom. Besides introducing it to new students, *the tour serves as a refresher not only for returning students, but also for teachers*. "Everyone needs to revisit the process," Darleen says, "especially those who've been away on vacation. It is so easy to slip back into old habits. The tour serves as a reminder for everyone." Darleen has created a student mentor program. Among those students who have been through her RTC and have been successful at making plans and succeeding in school, she selects some to help other students create successful plans. This is particularly useful when working with bilingual children.

Darleen initially had set the number of questions students could ask while in the RTC, due to the fact that students kept raising their hands to ask questions, thus creating disruptions in the RTC. Realizing that this process wasn't compatible with the RTP's theoretical base, perceptual control theory (PCT), since it was an attempt to control students, she changed the process. Students now have to write out their questions, prioritizing them by importance, and leave the lists on their desks. Darleen periodically checks their lists of questions, answering only the first few on each list. This has dramatically reduced the number of questions asked, eliminating the disruption to the RTC. Darleen also worked out a plan with Barbara Redmond, Clarendon's school secretary, for children who enroll during the school year. After a child's parents have enrolled the child, both parents and child are given a tour of the RTC and the process is explained. "This is a prevention program that Barbara and I worked out," Darleen explains.

Nola Johnson, the RTC teacher at Solano Elementary School, developed an evaluation form for students who had been to the RTC, had made plans, and had continued to disrupt. Obviously, their plans were not effective. This form helps students evaluate their previous plans to identify what is working and what is not working. In this way, students gain information that will help them write and implement more successful plans.

Often, after having read *Book One* and being introduced to the program, a school faculty member will volunteer for the job. If this volunteer already has rapport and credibility with colleagues, this assures classroom teacher cooperation with her in the new role as RTC teacher. A good working relationship with other members of the staff will already have been established. Carol Sullivan, at Maryvale High School, is just such an example. Not only did she work well with her peers, but she knew how to work with the teenagers in this very tough, urban environment. She, like Darleen, is among the best I've ever watched. She keeps a very "tight" room, where the atmosphere is like a library, and where students are sitting quietly at their carrels, staying to themselves and not disturbing others. Carol works well with the students, who soon learn not to take advantage of her kind, but very firm, approach.

In Carol's classroom, the students are treated as they would be in any other room. After the first disruption, they are asked the RTP questions. The students are well aware of the consequences when they continue to disrupt. Carol has them read and sign a list of the RTC rules and the consequences when they first enter the room. This is a very tough, inner-city high school, where a second disruption means they've chosen to leave. One of the eight security officers escorts the student to a restricted area until school is dismissed. The student is informed that her classes are closed to her, and that to return to class, she must come back to school with a parent. She must then work out a plan with the RTC teacher, with the parent present, to re-enter the school, which means that she first returns to the RTC and demonstrates responsibility there. Then she makes another plan to re-enter her other classes, where she continues to follow the rules, respecting the rights of both the teacher and her peers.

At Maryvale, upon returning to school, the student is put on "earn-all." This is a method of returning to class that was created by LeEdna Custer-Knight at Clarendon Elementary School. With earn-all, returning students aren't mainstreamed into all of their classes at once. They have to "earn" back the privilege of being in class. Working with Carol, a returning student creates a prioritized list of her classes. The first class listed is the one where the student thinks she will most likely succeed. The last class is the one where she thinks she is least likely to succeed. The student then returns to the first class on the earn-all monitor sheet and demonstrates her ability and willingness to succeed. The remainder of the day she'll spend in the RTC. Once she has sufficiently shown that she can behave responsibly in the easiest class, she'll go to the next one on the list. After the student demonstrates that she can handle responsibility in the first class she's chosen, she begins to build the necessary self-confidence in her ability to succeed. And she has done it without any threats or coercion. In the meantime, the rest of the students have been learning and the teachers have been teaching without the usual disruptions that restrict learning and teaching time. In order to keep up with her class work, the student continues to complete the school work assigned in her classes while in the RTC. It generally takes a week for her to earn back all of her classes.

At Maryvale, the faculty thinks the RTC is so critical to the process that, when Carol is absent for any reason, a substitute teacher is never assigned to this room. Instead, an experienced and trained teacher takes over the RTC, assuring its continued success. A substitute is then assigned to the replacement teacher's classroom.

If there is no volunteer from the faculty for the RTC teacher's position, one has to be hired from outside the school. My late friend Joe Sierzenga had a good suggestion. He asked all those interested in the position to read *Book One* and to come in with a plan as to how they were going to conduct the room.

Another value of the RTC was realized by Rod Bond, head teacher at Lukachukai Boarding School on the Navajo Reservation in northern Arizona. He and the school counselor, Lu Tallbull, who acted as RTC teacher until the process was safely established, worked as a team to build an excellent program. They had the support and active participation of most staff. Halfway through the year, 20 children who had caused major problems in other schools were sent to Lukachukai. Rod and Lu soon learned the best way to mainstream children into the school is to first assign them to the RTC and *slowly work them into the classrooms*, using the earn-all process. Bringing them into the classroom slowly helped students build the necessary confidence they needed to be successful from the very beginning. They weren't placed into situations that they could not handle. The new students had to earn their way into the classrooms, demonstrating their respect for the rules and for the rights of the teachers and the other students.

One of the best physical set-ups for the RTC is at Vulture Peak Middle School in Wickenburg, Arizona, where Mike Helminski is principal. Alondra Roehler, the aide, sits next to the door, where children check in. The desks in this classroom-size room are faced toward the wall, in study carrels. Suzanne Winzeler, the RTC teacher, sits to the left of the aide. In front of her is an enclosed portion of the room for private work with children who need help with their plans. Both the teacher and the aide can see all of the children. Any student who disrupts for a second time, and thus refuses to follow the rules in the RTC, is automatically taken home by Mike. And, according to Mike, it took a lot of adjusting on his part when he was asked by Suzanne to take a student home. Prior to RTP, he had always reviewed the problem and made the decision himself. From what I've been told by many educators, administrators tend to compromise the decisions of their staff, thus weakening the teachers' authority. This process respects the decisions of everyone, students and teachers. So now Mike has to respect the decisions of Suzanne, demonstrating not only his confidence in her but in how the process should work.

Another school that has demonstrated exceptional use of the program is in the Combs School District in Queen Creek, Arizona. During one of my visits, Don Nelson, the superintendent and principal, took me to the RTC, where Nancy Hatch, the RTC teacher, was helping a student work on a plan. There were a number of other students who, after disrupting, had chosen to go to the RTC. They were sitting quietly at study carrels. Others were there to "chill out," which meant they had asked to go to the RTC because they had gotten angry and needed a place to cool off rather than get in trouble. Also, several students were there to study. It seems that they lived in highly dysfunctional homes, where they couldn't study even if they wanted. When given the chance, these students took advantage of the opportunity for extra study time. Don worked with their teachers and created some time during the school day for doing their homework. Don works closely with Nancy, making sure that the RTC is utilized to the fullest extent.

At Squaw Peak Elementary School in the Creighton Elementary School District in Phoenix, where Kathy Tegarden is principal, staff came up with a way of putting parents of disruptive children more at ease. Mark Yslas, who is assistant principal, and Briley Culton, the RTC teacher, worked out a plan to help parents develop a better understanding of the process. When parents come to pick up their child who has disrupted in the RTC and has thus chosen to go home, Briley offers to "show" the parents the RTC. Briley explains that "many people are visual, like I am, and when the parents enter the room, I introduce them to the RTC aides, show them the posted rules, explain the various forms, and they observe the other children sitting quietly, working on their plans or doing their homework. They'd see it as a classroom, not as punishment, and they seemed to become more accepting of the program." And this takes us to the most important position of all: the administrator.

Sadly, some of the schools mentioned in this chapter and the rest of the book are no longer using RTP. The administrators moved on or, even after several years of success, decided to "improve" on the process—which destroyed it. RTC teachers lost the "front office" support and team relationships so necessary to the success of the process. In other cases, administrators were interested only in RTP, not PCT, the underlying theory that protects the integrity of the process. Thus, slowly but surely, cause-effect thinking began to work its way back into various areas of the schools. A new playground supervisor would establish her own style of "dealing with those kids." Or newly hired teachers, fresh from cause-effect training, would attempt to use the RTC as a dumping ground or detention center for misbehaving students. Or new administrators would have higher priorities. As one superintendent told a principal who had successfully reduced school suspensions by 60% in one year, "Now that you've got this school under control, when are you going to get rid of 'that' room?"

For an up-to-date list of certified schools, check the RTP web page, www.respthink.com.

Chapter 5
An Administrator
Must Drive the Process

Nothing is more important to this process than a respected administrator who *understands the process, wants it to succeed, and continually works with and supports the RTC teacher, as well as the rest of the faculty and staff, to make sure it does succeed.* The RTC teacher and administrator, with constant input from the rest of the staff, must work as a team, always looking for ways to upgrade the process and to make it more efficient. More importantly, they must be looking for breakdowns.

I was more than fortunate when I was asked to create my model at Clarendon in 1994. Del Merrill, the principal, gave the model his strong support and encouragement. On several occasions, he had to defend it from critics outside the school. There were also two outstanding educators who drove the process. The first was George Venetis, who worked as assistant principal half-time at Clarendon Elementary School and half-time at Solano Elementary School, both in the Osborn School District in Phoenix. The other was LeEdna Custer-Knight, who worked at Clarendon as the school psychologist. I have never met two more dedicated and caring educators in my life. LeEdna spent time with faculty, teaching and encouraging the use of the process, demonstrating and conducting student discussions in classrooms, and supporting, along with George, Darleen Martin, the RTC teacher. In only a few schools that are attempting this process have I found two staff who work as a team with the RTC teacher. Even today, long after the process was initiated, all three are still looking for ways to improve it and expand it more and more into the educational process. It is the ideal way for the process to develop and grow.

Teachers Who Refuse to Use the Process

After talking with children who are in the RTC, I can give you a good estimate of the percentage of teachers who are using the process. Recently, I visited a school's RTC and worked with three children in succession whose teachers had "told" them to get out and go to the RTC. A fourth child, according to the RTC teacher, was arbitrarily sent to the room until the child's teacher decided when he would be allowed to return. All of those actions by the teachers were completely against RTP. Yet the people at this school believed that they were using the process correctly. Their idea of an RTC was to use it as a detention center. Obviously, students could simply claim that a teacher "never asked them the questions." However, according to Darleen Martin, the RTC teacher at Clarendon, "It is only the occasional students with whom I've worked who will lie about whether or not their teachers have used the process."

No one has demonstrated better skill in dealing with teachers who refuse to use the process and are still choosing to try to control their students than George Venetis. George suggests that administrators should always deal with staff in the same way they deal with students, namely with a calm, respectful, and curious approach. Teachers who insist on controlling their students should be asked the following. The first question George usually asks is "Who's responsible for what the student does?" Then he follows with "When you choose to take responsibility for controlling your students rather than allowing them to be responsible for their own actions, are you also choosing to be accountable for their actions and the choices they make?" He concludes with "Is that what you want?"

The responsible thinking classroom is not a detention center. It is designed as an alternative choice for students who, for whatever reasons, refuse to follow the rules of wherever they are. It is a place where, when they're ready, they can work on plans to help them deal effectively with their problems without infringing on the rights of others. In other words, students, not teachers, are being held accountable for the choices they make.

Another question George suggests for the teacher who is not using the process is "If you're taking responsibility for the student's actions based on what you do to him, do you really think the RTC is the right place for him to go?" And "Do you think you should be allowed to send him to the RTC, when this classroom is not designed for your program and for the way you're dealing with students?" And then "If you're trying to control the student, who makes the plan for the child's future choices and the actions that follow, you or the student?" Other questions might be these: "Are you trying to control him to teach him compliance, or to learn to think for himself?" "Where in your program are you teaching him to think for himself, to make effective plans to deal with his future conflicts?"

Teachers who do not use the process, but insist on trying to control a student's behavior, refuse to take responsibility for the student's misconduct in their classroom. They hold a student accountable for not being able to control his behavior. If the particular attempt by a teacher reduces the classroom disruption, the teacher takes credit. If, on the other hand, disruption escalates, then the student is held accountable. Yet, many of these same teachers hold a student accountable for their not being able to control the child's behavior. If a classroom teacher is going to place a child outside her room for disrupting her class, when she allows the child to re-enter the classroom, she will still hold him accountable for what he does. If she puts his name on the board, takes away points, gives him detention or extra homework, has him stand in the corner, or sends him to the principal's office, all of these actions by the teacher are attempts to control actions of the student. How can the student be held accountable for the teacher's actions? Is it what the teacher did to the student that was ineffective, or did the child fail? These are questions that should be asked when teachers put themselves in the position of trying to control students.

If a teacher refuses to take part in RTP and continues to "do" things to a student to get her to behave, is he not making a deliberate choice to control the student in a specific way? If so, is the teacher not also responsible for the way the student reacts to what he is doing to the student?

Educators can't have it both ways. To take credit for being able to control a student when he follows the rules and yet hold this same student accountable for disruption doesn't make sense. If they insist on trying to control a student's behavior, then educators must be held accountable for how the student reacts when being controlled. If, on the other hand, as perceptual control theory teaches, each student is responsible individually for what he does, then the educator must respect the student and how he is designed, and use the process.

When training a school faculty, I've asked participants, "Can I control what you do?" or "Can I make you do what you don't want to do?" The answer is always the same: "No." Then I ask, "What would happen if I tried to make you stand in the corner of the room with your face against the wall?" I get a variety of answers, but they all suggest resistance, with possible violence and anger. Then I ask, "Are we designed the same as children, with the same brain structure?" The answer comes back, "Yes." Then I ask, "If I can't control you as a human being, and I'd only cause problems if I'd try, does it make sense to control children?" followed by "Do you blame children for reacting the way they do when you try to control them?" Then I think of what my friend, George Venetis, would say. He'd look at me with that knowing smile of his and say, "Case closed!"

Teachers who refuse to participate in the process and "send" their students to the RTC can make difficulties for both the students and the RTC teacher. The students enter the RTC with the perception that they are being punished for their actions. When the RTC teacher offers to help one of these students with his problem, the student might claim that the problem is with the teacher who made the decision to remove him from class, and who will decide when he can return. In this case, what reason is there for the student to think about what he is doing or to write a plan? The purpose of the room makes no sense to the student. That purpose is in conflict with the actions of his classroom teacher. His teacher should be asked, "Is the RTC appropriate to your way of dealing with students?"

Other questions for such teachers could include: "If you want students to be responsible, how is doing something to them going to create within them the responsible thinking for which you are looking?" "If you're doing all of the manipulating and controlling, what are children learning?" "How do they learn to take responsibility by what you are doing to them?" "Who's doing most of the work, and who's doing most of the thinking?" "Where are they being taught to think for themselves, to make plans?" "Are you trying to control them so that they will just be compliant, or are they learning to think for themselves?"

Teachers want administrative support, and rightly so. However, when they decide not to use the responsible thinking process and to continue to try to control their students, they put the administrator in an awkward situation when dealing with parents. Many parents want the teacher and administrator to be responsible and accountable for their child's behavior. The question an administrator might ask the teacher who is not using the process is "If you choose to try to control the child and not use RTP, then have you not also chosen to be accountable to the parents for their child's behavior?" In other words, "If you choose to control children, and you're taking responsibility for their actions, then are you not responsible to the parents for their children's actions in your classroom?" The real problem with teachers who refuse to use the process is that they still expect the administrator to defend their actions when they run contrary to the process. How can an administrator defend the teacher or other staff member in such a situation? If a staff member chooses to be accountable, then all that the administrator can do is hold the employee accountable for the choices they've made. What other choice does the administrator have?

The administrator must constantly be aware of what is happening in the RTC and whether classroom teachers and other members of the staff are following the process. (The specific role of the administrators in schools where the process is successful is covered in much more detail in Chapter 8.) The administrator continually needs to review the various concerns of the faculty, to deal with their questions, and to help align everyone's ideas of how things should be.

From the beginning, teachers need support as they learn the process. It is critical that there should be frequent faculty meetings, sharing of problems and concerns as well as solutions, encouraging those who seem to have doubts, and updating everyone as to the progress of the process. Also, there should be immediate discussions held with individual teachers and staff who have gone back to the old way of "yelling and telling" or have re-introduced cause-effect thinking. Once RTP is underway, and everyone is comfortable with the process, the faculty and staff should meet every three to four weeks, constantly evaluating their progress.

It is absolutely critical that the administrator support the decisions of the RTC teacher. Without that support and team effort, the RTC teacher is many times left out on a limb, and the whole process begins to break down and fall apart. So, without continued administrative support, the process will become mediocre at best. The RTC will turn into a holding tank for disruptive children, where children are verbally beaten up and humiliated.

In many schools, I've seen initial excitement for RTP turn into a desperate struggle to keep anything that resembles RTP alive. Without an administrator who really believes in the process, understands it, drives it, and continually supports the teachers, nothing else will bring the process to the point where students are happy and learning, teachers are relaxed and teaching, and parents are proud of the school.

And what about those teachers who have refused to use the process? They have given up their right to use the RTC. Since the administrator is part of the process, those same teachers must deal directly with the parents of their students.

Chapter 6
Unexpected Developments

The Responsible Thinking Process is intended to replace traditional discipline programs based on the cause-effect model, with detention, suspension, giving and taking away points, or delivering rewards and punishments, all designed to do something to the student in order to create the proper action or behavior in response. These approaches are totally inconsistent with the theoretical basis of RTP, perceptual control theory (PCT), which is explained in Chapter 7, A Solid Basis For RTP. PCT recognizes that every person behaves in order to make some of her experiences in the world be the way she wants them to be. Drawing on the ideas in PCT, RTP was created to replace ineffective cause-effect approaches. I've identified some unexpected consequences that might occur when a school tries to implement RTP. Some of these consequences can prevent the process from ever working. Others occur after the process is in place, revealing problems that were previously hidden or unanticipated.

Some of the problems that can prevent the process from working were described above. Sometimes the administrator assigned to drive the process does not carry out that role. Other times, the person who should run the RTC fails in that role. Sometimes too few of the faculty buy into the process or become discouraged and quit following it. Alone, any one of these problems might prevent RTP from working; however, without an administrator who believes in the process, understands it, continually supports the teachers by helping them refine their skills, and works as a team with the RTC teacher, RTP is doomed.

One thing that is common throughout all of the schools where I've worked is the need to define what a disruption is and the terms used to label certain offenses. For example, if the school board mandates a five-day suspension for a physical assault, then what might be to one teacher shoving, and to another fighting, to a third might be a physical assault. It is critical that there be agreement as to what constitutes a disruption. Certainly, human nature being the way it is, teachers, parents, and administrators are going to vary in the way they work with RTP, but there should be a high degree of consistency, especially when it comes to defining terms used to describe the various kinds of disruptions.

Sometimes, when the process is working very well, problems that were previously hidden, or were unanticipated, come to light. For example, in the beginning, it is not unusual for large numbers of students to choose to go to the RTC. This is not necessarily bad. Often, what is happening is simply that many students whose disruptions previously were tolerated by teachers now go to the RTC. Also, teachers who had hesitated to see their students leave their classrooms for discipline problems, because they would be held accountable for having "failed to control the behavior of their students," no longer feel threatened when students choose to go to the RTC. It once happened that an entire class decided to disrupt and go to the RTC, simply to test the program or to "check out" the RTC. In that case, the assistant principal told the class that they had lost their privilege of using the RTC and now had a choice of going directly home or working out individual plans for resolving the problem. They settled down and worked on their plans.

After the initial "rush" of students going to the RTC, the level of disruptions in a school usually goes down. When it does, staff members sometimes notice that certain individual students make repeated trips to the RTC. What happens after they notice the "repeaters" is critical to the survival of the process. For example, in some schools, staff members decide that the repeaters are proof that the Responsible Thinking Process is not working, and they overlay it with elements of traditional cause-effect discipline programs. They believe that these strategies will allow them to gain control over the behavior of the repeaters. I'm constantly amazed when I hear of a return to old habits at a site where RTP has failed. I've asked teachers, "Did that work in the past?" The answer generally is "Well, no, but we've got to do something." Yet in every one of the schools where these elements have been added, RTP has subsequently failed or has been in serious trouble.

An overlay, or parallel process, that I have seen in some schools occurs when a student becomes a "chronic problem," and many teachers want to return to a traditional cause-effect intervention. They add little punishments of their own, such as having the student sit on the floor outside the classroom, keeping the child in class after school, or penalizing the entire class because of the actions of one student. All of this is highly antagonistic to PCT and is totally against the process to which the teachers have committed. In RTP, the student decides when to leave the RTC. Another example of an overlay is when private counselors suggest that the classroom teacher of their student-client use reward or punishment programs that run counter to PCT and RTP.

Interestingly, repeaters can reveal problems with what seems to be RTP, but, in reality, *are problems with the way the process is being applied, not with its core assumptions*. The way to deal with these problems is to examine how the process is being applied and what is blocking the process. For example, a student might become a repeater when staff members do not help him prepare a plan that is appropriate to his succeeding, but that more or less sets him up to fail. Or perhaps the classroom teacher does not actively negotiate with the student when she comes from the RTC, submits a plan to the teacher, and is ready to work out a way to resolve her problem. A review of the negotiating techniques with the teacher might be helpful. These kinds of problems require simple changes in how teachers apply the process. Other problems might suggest that the teacher needs to learn new skills. All problems like these should be addressed by the administrator who drives the process.

Even when RTP is working well, repeaters often reveal problems, not with RTP, but with other influences in their lives. Some students choose to go to the RTC because they perceive it as a calmer place than the classroom they left, or perhaps they perceive it as more stable and predictable. In short, they need a quiet place to calm down, to gather some strength. Some choose to go to the RTC because they perceive the teacher there as more friendly to them than the one in the classroom they left, or as more caring or fair. At a school in Michigan during the bitterly cold months in the winter, increased numbers of students found ways to choose the RTC rather than the playground. In each of these cases, teachers and administrators realized that students who made repeated visits to the RTC were using it as a way to control their perceptions or experiences. They did not view the students themselves, or their visits to the RTC, or their teachers as the problems. *Instead, the staff tried to discover which problems the students were trying to solve for themselves, then helped the children resolve their own problems.* As Rod Bond at Lukachukai Boarding School observed, "This process allows our staff to work with the most difficult children, but we must stick with the process. It just takes longer in some cases. And it definitely takes patience."

In Joe Sierzenga's school in Michigan, he found many students came from homes so dysfunctional that even if they wanted to study, the home environment made it impossible. Joe arranged time during school for them to use the RTC for studying. He allowed some of the students to use the RTC as a place to sleep or just to calm down.

In every school where RTP is working well, there are fewer disruptions than before, and the staff members find that they can more easily identify and help students who have serious needs. Often, those students are among the repeaters. For example, some of them are students who come from seriously dysfunctional homes, or who have emotional or relational problems, or who have serious learning difficulties. Once again, the staff members do not view a student's repeated visits to the RTC as a problem in its own right, *but as sign that the student needs special help*.

This special help is called an *intervention team*, which evolved out of the experiences of many educators who have helped to build RTP. Two of those educators, Tim and Margaret Carey of Brisbane, Australia, have written an excellent chapter on the use of intervention teams (see page 66).

Chapter 7
A Solid Basis For RTP

W. Thomas Bourbon, Ph.D.
Perceptual Control Theorist
Rochelle, Texas

I've asked my friend, Tom Bourbon, to write this chapter. For many years after William T. Powers developed PCT as a theory of behavior, Tom was one of the few scientists in the world who conducted experimental studies, wrote working computer models to test PCT, and published the results in scientific journals. After receiving a grant, he joined me in 1995 to research RTP and to help me build more integrity into the process. Together, we have visited schools in 15 states, Australia, and Singapore.—Ed Ford

Ed Ford developed the Responsible Thinking Process (RTP) as a way to teach children how to achieve their own ends, without interfering with other people who are also trying to achieve theirs. In RTP, Ed embraced the fact that people always behave to make some of their experiences of the world be the way they want them to be; they act to control their own perceptions. The only theory I know of that explains how people control their experiences is perceptual control theory (PCT), developed by William T. Powers, starting in the 1950s. Ed Ford has tried to make RTP consistent with the ideas in PCT.

Three Ds: Disturbance, Disruption, and Discipline

A person who controls her perceptions *must* act or behave in order to affect things in the world around her.

She *must* push and pull on things, or affect them in some other physical way. She must change some things and make other things remain the same. But there are many other influences in the world that can affect the same things as she can. If anything or anyone else disturbs her ability to make perceptions be the way she thinks they "should be," she will oppose the effects of that disturbance. The person who wants to drive from home to work must continually act on the steering wheel, moving it any ways necessary to oppose the disturbing effects of crosswinds, bumps in the road, and poor tire alignment, to keep the view out the windshield changing so that he sees "progress along the road to work." The person who wants to see a knot in a rubber band remain over a dot on the blackboard must pull continually on one end of the rubber band to oppose disturbances due to another person pulling on the other end, as explained by Ed Ford on page 5 of his book *Freedom from Stress*. The student who wants to feel "accepted" by certain fellow students must vary her actions so she always sees the others treating her in a way she calls "acceptance." In each case, the person acts on the world to make what "is perceived" match what he thinks "should be perceived," so his experiences become what he wants them to be.

Whenever several people are physically close together, such as at school, at work, at home, playing a game, or working on a project, and all of them control their own experiences, it is inevitable that, sooner or later, one or more of them will affect part of the world in a way that disturbs the experiences of others. Often, that kind of disturbance is unintentional, but sometimes a person does it on purpose. Whichever is the case, people whose control is disturbed by someone else often oppose whoever creates the disturbance. When people are close together, occasional disturbances and opposition to them are natural and unavoidable, but when that kind of interaction occurs in school, it is often called "disruption," and the person who is identified as a "disrupter" is "disciplined."

In traditional discipline programs, students are often

treated like objects that can be controlled by what happens around them, much the way the temperature of a rock is controlled by cycles of dark and daylight, the seasons, and the weather. This is a classic example of a "cause-effect" relationship, where something that happens to an object causes the object to change in a specific way. *But even something as basic as a child's internal body temperature is not controlled that way by the environment. A child is a living control system and keeps her own internal temperature constant, in spite of what goes on in the environment.* A person controls his body temperature by actions, some "automatic," others intentional, that oppose the effects of disturbances from the environment. If the environment doesn't even control a student's body temperature, how likely is it that the same environment, in the guise of a teacher or parent or assistant principal, controls the student's attitudes, thoughts, emotions, and actions? Not very likely!

The Dance of Control and Counter-Control

A teacher who tries to discipline a student and control her behavior unwittingly becomes a disturbance to the student's perceptions, and the student will then oppose the teacher's actions. The *harder* the teacher tries to control the student's behavior, the easier it is for her to disturb the teacher in return and *counter-control* his behavior. Imagine a very simple example. The teacher decides he will "get in the face" of a disrupting student. When the student sees him standing directly in front of her, she feels uncomfortable; he is standing closer than the student likes people to stand. To oppose that disturbance, she backs away from him, a move he might incorrectly interpret as the student "backing down." If he decides to press the issue with the student, he might step forward to keep the gap between them closed. If he continues to advance, and the student keeps backing away, he might believe he is "really putting her in her place."

He might be completely wrong. If the student has noticed that every time she backs away, the teacher advances, she can move from "being controlled by the teacher" to "counter-controlling the teacher." For example, if she wants to lead the teacher around the room, all she has to do is keep backing in the direction she wants to see him going. The dance is underway! The teacher sees the student doing what he wants her to do; the student sees the teacher doing what she wants him to do. The teacher thought he was "putting her in her place," but now the student can literally "put him" nearly any place she wants. Which of them do you think is smiling?

Trying Harder: Turning Up the Gain

When one perceptual control system tries to control the actions of another, counter-control like that in the previous example is *always* possible. That is why people who try to use traditional discipline programs to control students' actions *nearly always* feel like they are being "yanked around" by the students. They are.

When a person acts to eliminate "perceptual error," which is the difference between his intended perception and his present perception, he acts like a "control system." An interesting fact about a control system is that if you increase its "gain," then when it experiences the same amount of perceptual error, the system will produce a more vigorous "output." For example, a teacher might decide to "turn up his gain" and try harder to control a student. If he does, then for the same amount of difference between what the teacher *wants to see* the student doing and what he *actually sees* her doing, he will act more vigorously to try to "make her behave."

Teachers might decide to try harder, or do more, to control the "behavior" of making repeated visits to the RTC. The teachers have the same desired perceptions as before (to see students not make repeated visits), but they have "turned up the gain" (trying harder to make them not return). Those teachers beg more passionately and yell more loudly than before. They adopt more coercive measures. They contrive more intricate contingencies and more outlandish strategies. In every case, the result is likely to be the same: students will quickly discover that it is easier than ever before to counter-control the teachers. That is always a possibility whenever one control system tries to control the actions of another, and it is almost guaranteed to happen when a teacher "turns up the gain."

The Responsible Thinking Process and PCT

The greatest success with RTP comes when teachers understand that each person controls his or her own experiences. Teachers who know that fact usually stop trying to control students' behavior. They are no longer subject to counter-control by their students, and they feel a great sense of relief. Rather than trying to control students' behavior, teachers start helping them learn how to think their way through situations where they formerly "disrupted." The teachers know they cannot use traditional methods for "cognitive restructuring" to put ideas like "fairness," "respect," or "justice" into students' heads, but they can help students experience conditions that are labeled by those words. After they experience those conditions with RTP, students themselves can say what they mean and why they are important.

RTP is not something you "do to" students to "make them behave," once and for all. No discipline process can eliminate the fact that, at some time or another, each of us disturbs someone else, while we all go about the business of controlling our own experiences. But in schools where the Responsible Thinking Process is working well, both students and staff learn to think about their plans and actions, so that when they act to control their own experiences, they will minimize the chances that they disturb others. That is the best we can do.

Chapter 8
What Everyone's Expected to Do

Probably the single most important aspect of the process is to define everyone's role. When I first built the model at Clarendon, I couldn't have defined the roles. I was first trying to define the process. Fortunately, I had the kind of people around me who didn't need to have their jobs defined. George, LeEdna, and Darleen just did what they thought best, and at weekly staff meetings, as we worked through the various problems and concerns, everyone just adjusted what they did to make the process work.

As other schools attempted to implement the process, much of what we had assimilated became a part of our daily routine and needed to be defined. What George, LeEdna, and Darleen were doing was what naturally evolved as the process was being created. Now they had to step back from their jobs and look at what they had been doing. For those who wanted to implement the process, there was now a need to define the various jobs that were essential to the success of RTP.

The following, then, are the roles of the various school personnel involved in the Responsible Thinking Process.

1. The Administrator

a. The school administrator who drives the process must be respected and trusted by the staff and must be perceived as understanding the theory and the process.

b. The administrator needs to become familiar with RTP by having read and re-read current materials and books on the process. He needs to have a basic understanding of perceptual control theory (PCT) by having read the current literature and by having had sufficient training from those recommended by RTP, Inc. To protect the integrity of RTP, he must have a very clear understanding of PCT. This is critical to his role.

c. To help the staff keep their ideas about RTP and PCT aligned, the administrator should organize and facilitate weekly meetings with the entire staff during the first few months. At these meetings, the staff should review current issues needing solutions, resolve any misunderstandings, be presented with information concerning changes in the process or in forms, and create uniformity in the way the staff use terms and forms to describe the various actions of the students. Once the program is running smoothly, staff meetings should be held at least once every three weeks.

d. The administrator reviews the effectiveness of the process by studying RTC data and by talking with students, the RTC teacher, school staff, and parents. He should spend no less than 20 minutes a day in the RTC.

e. The administrator creates a "team" atmosphere with the RTC teacher. They constantly review and update the process and provide assistance and support to the rest of the staff. The administrator, rather than the RTC teacher, deals with staff members who refuse to follow the process. The administrator, using the questioning techniques with his staff, should deal with accountability, not blame, in a supportive way.

f. When the RTC teacher reports that a student has broken the rules and chosen to go home, the administrator follows the process and calls the parents to come and pick up their child. If there is no car available, the child is taken home by two people from the school. At some schools, where false phone numbers and/or addresses have been given, the children are taken to where a parent works. And no parent should be allowed to re-admit their child without a correct address and phone number, including an additional emergency number for when the parents cannot be reached by phone. Similarly, it is the responsibility of the administrator, not the RTC teacher, to deal with serious acts of student misconduct. The administrator will meet with the student and determine, based on school board policy, whether in-school or out-of-school suspension is required. Also, when the RTC teacher reports that a student has been in the classroom for one full day and has refused to make a plan to resolve his problem, the administrator schedules an intervention team meeting. (See responsibilities of intervention team below.)

g. The administrator must use the RTP questioning techniques not only with students and staff, but also with parents. When a student returns with her parents after being suspended or after having chosen to leave the RTC and go home, the administrator should meet with the student, her parents, and the RTC teacher to determine whether the student is ready to return to school and create a plan for re-entry into her classes.

h. The administrator annually assesses and evaluates the process. This initially includes providing an assessment form for staff to fill out at the conclusion of the first year. The following year, it is strongly recommended that those involved in the process design and implement an assessment form for parents and students.

i. The administrator continues to monitor the process to assure no alternative or parallel programs are used which conflict with PCT and RTP. All modifications, overlays, and additions to RTP must be approved by the administrator and must be consistent with PCT.

j. The administrator must regularly conduct and observe classroom discussions. (See *Discipline for Home and School, Book One*, Chapter 6, bottom of page 23.)

k. The administrator continually looks for funds to finance staff training and the RTC.

2. *The Responsible Thinking Classroom Teacher*

a. The RTC teacher must have a basic understanding of the process and PCT, and a clear understanding of the administration of the RTC. The RTC teacher assists the administrator in driving the process.

b. The RTC teacher needs to become familiar with RTP by having read and re-read current materials and books on the process; needs to have a basic understanding of perceptual control theory by having read the current literature and by having taken the proper training from someone recommended by RTP, Inc.; and needs to have a clear understanding of everyone's role in the process.

c. The RTC teacher uses and models the process in the responsible thinking classroom by using the RTP questions; assigning each student to a specific desk; making sure the students understand and follow the RTC rules and options; assisting students when they decide they are ready to work on their plans or on school work; reviewing a student's previous plans as they relate to the present one and suggesting various interventions when appropriate; reviewing student monitor sheets; reviewing the earn-all list and monitoring students' progress; notifying the classroom teacher when a student has an acceptable plan and is ready to negotiate; developing and revising student daily calendars; and working cooperatively with the RTC aide.

d. The RTC teacher works with staff to modify and adjust student programs, plans, and schedules when needed; works with classroom teachers to set up a schedule for when teachers can negotiate with students; notifies the administrator when a teacher does not deal with a student in a timely fashion or does not follow the process; and collects class assignments from each teacher.

e. When a student refuses to follow the rules in the RTC and chooses to go home, the RTC teacher immediately notifies the administrator. Any time a student commits a serious act of misconduct according to district policy, the RTC teacher immediately reports the offense to the administrator. The RTC teacher notifies the administrator of any student who, after one full day in the RTC, still does not work out a plan to resolve the problem.

f. The RTC teacher helps the administrator organize and

facilitate discussion groups of school staff; works with the administrator to monitor and evaluate the RTC aide; continually monitors and adjusts the process within the RTC, including the revision of forms and rules; and is responsible for the overall appearance of the RTC.

g. When there is no RTC aide, the RTC teacher assumes the aide's responsibilities.

3. The Responsible Thinking Classroom Aide

a. The aide reports directly to the RTC teacher.

b. The aide must have read *Discipline for Home and School, Book One*, this book, and other appropriate material, have a basic understanding of the process, and know the workings of the RTC.

c. The aide, who is responsible for all RTC clerical work, helps the teacher screen referrals to the room, keeps a daily log of students, and maintains all student discipline records, making copies when necessary. The aide prepares letters to parents, records the number of referrals to the RTC, and makes a monthly report to the proper channels.

d. The aide assists the RTC teacher in assigning seats and monitoring the room.

e. When the RTC teacher is absent for any reason, and no other teacher has taken her place, the aide should temporarily assume the responsibilities of the teacher.

4. The Classroom Teacher

a. The teacher must follow the process, needs to become familiar with RTP by having read and re-read current materials and books on the process, and needs to have a basic understanding of perceptual control theory by having read the current literature and having taken the proper training from someone recommended by RTP, Inc.

b. The teacher must use the RTP questioning techniques when dealing with students. After the teacher asks the RTP questions, if a student continues to break the rules, the child has chosen to go to the RTC, and the teacher fills out the student referral form and sends the child with the form. Sometimes the teacher might send the RTC referral form with another student.

c. The teacher gives the RTC teacher a copy of her schedule, which will include the times she is available to negotiate with students.

d. The teacher will negotiate at his earliest available scheduled time. The student should be given adequate time to discuss the plan, and when it is not acceptable, the teacher should offer alternative suggestions. This student-teacher negotiating time is an excellent way for teachers to have one-on-one quality time with their students. As was mentioned in *Book One* (Chapter 6), quality time creates the kind of relational strength from which children will more likely allow the adult the necessary access needed to resolve in a calm and respectful way the various conflicts which occur.

e. The teacher maintains a file of all acceptable plans. If a plan is revised during negotiations, the classroom teacher sees to it that the RTC teacher gets a copy.

f. All staff members should follow the process wherever they see disruption.

g. Teachers will assist students with their monitor sheets.

h. Teachers will conduct classroom discussions on a regular basis, but no less than once a week. The purpose of these discussions is the development of social skills of the children. As students learn to respect what other children say, especially differing opinions, they gradually learn to respect the speakers. (See *Book One*, Chapter 6, bottom of page 23.)

5. *The Intervention Team*

(Chapter 14, by Tim and Margaret Carey, looks in detail at the intervention team.)

a. The perfect role for a school counselor would be as head of the intervention team. In many schools, the counselor's role is filled by the principal, assistant principal, social worker, psychologist, or a combination of staff. The counselor should have a good working knowledge of RTP and a clear understanding of PCT. The counselor should work closely with the RTC teacher and should regularly spend time in the RTC, working with the students (especially the more disruptive students).

b. The purpose of this team is to review current data and to make recommendations to help the student succeed.

c. This team includes the administrator who drives the process, the RTC teacher, the student's teachers, the child's parents, and appropriate support personnel, such as the school psychologist, school counselor, or social worker.

d. This team meets when no school interventions or student plans have worked, as sometimes happens with a "chronically disruptive child." It also meets when a child has remained in the RTC for more than one full day, refusing to work at resolving his problem. As Edwin Snyder, principal of Boyne City Elementary School, wisely remarked, "I see the repeater as a challenge and as someone needing help, not as a child who needs more punishment or more control."

6. All Staff Members

All staff members, especially those who come in contact in any way with students, including those working part-time at the school and those servicing the school, such as school bus drivers, cafeteria workers, playground supervisors, custodial staff, and especially school secretaries, should receive a copy of *Book One* and be trained in the process. They should be included in the regular staff meetings called by the administrator—the school secretaries especially, who, more than anyone else, are in daily contact with parents.

When anyone is left out of the training, that person could continue to experience disruption. Kent Roberts, an eighth grade teacher at Lukachukai Boarding School, observed,

"When the student can't disrupt and stay in the classroom, he often chooses 'the weakest link in the chain' to vent his anger or frustrations, which may be the school bus. When a teacher properly uses the process, the child learns to follow the rules. When the same student gets on a bus with a driver who doesn't use the process, the child might easily start to play his little games and disrupt." (See 1k above.)

Part 2. Avoiding and Solving Common Problems

Chapter 9
Setting the Stage for RTP

John Champlin
National Educator
Institute for Quality Learning
Scottsdale, Arizona

Many educators remind me of the incessant shoppers at Filene's basement in Boston, a notorious source of bargains: they are constantly seeking yet another program that promises relief from their ponderous ongoing problems.

When a program is embraced by a school district, there is always an imperative to ask the question, "Will our culture support it?" Culture is a series of pervasive relationships involving ways of thinking and behaving that result from people deciding "this is how we should do business here." The constraints of culture are too often overlooked or considered insufficiently. When a school district's culture is not "right," the introduction of new programs or new techniques simply will not succeed, regardless of their virtues. The culture must be changed *before* the programs are adopted.

An analogy illustrating this point is that of the farmer who plows and prepares his fields *prior* to planting. In our schools, we must create *pre-conditions* that allow at least a chance for successful change. Another analogy: I remember my high school biology teacher introducing the amoeba to the class. She dropped a particle onto a microscope slide. We watched an amoeba surround the particle, which disappeared. School culture is like an amoeba. It can surround good intentions and destroy them.

The Responsible Thinking Process abandons coercive

controlling by teachers as they work with children who are choosing their own behaviors. How far has *your* district come on its journey away from coercion? Most schools are filled with relationships that are controlling and coercive. Even though these behaviors fail to give staff what they claim they want, many continue to be coercive and controlling. It's as if they have tacitly agreed not to see that they are *not* getting what they claim to value. Each district needs to immerse itself in a serious examination of what staff are willing to do to get what they verbally claim they want. What they want and speak for *can* be had, but *not* by continuing to do what they have traditionally done.

An accompanying issue when introducing RTP is the changing role of the teacher. Traditionally, teachers have been positioned to prescribe behaviors and then to sit in judgment of the resulting behaviors. But with RTP, when a student comes back with a plan to negotiate his return to class, the role of the teacher is *not* that of the traditional adjudicator. This is a time when teacher-pupil engagement requires dialogue, probing, questioning, and reflection in a calm, respectful way about what it takes to make the plan work. While the pupil certainly has responsibility for the plan, the success of the plan to a great degree results from the teacher and student having talked through expectations and refinements. Teachers who miss the opportunity to dialogue and build better personal relationships with students lose significant opportunities. Too many students see teachers as adversaries. Dialoguing a plan is a great chance for connecting with each other. The difficulty lies in teachers playing a new role—dialoguing and sharing, rather than directing. It might seem an exaggeration, but there are few teachers who are comfortable in a more informal role with students. So there might be a real need to provide support and training to sharpen the required skills.

School staff who believe that problems can be resolved by sending a pupil to the principal for correction will find RTP challenging. Problems are the property and the responsibility of two persons, the staff member and the student. This creates a new spirit and new opportunities. Problem ownership by staff members as expressed in working through the RTP questions is an exceptional opportunity, but one not welcomed by those who enjoy being aloof and distant from students.

We all have seen attempted changes come and go—mostly go, because the culture did not accept new requirements. If you don't want to be surprised and disappointed when embracing RTP, then *plan* for its requirements; *plan* to prepare staff for its requirements. Change *can* and *must* be managed. The new process cannot survive in a hostile, unreceptive setting. But when we seek out problems and issues, we can prepare to solve them. So, the key is to *get ready* for RTP in your district.

Chapter 10
Arranging the
Responsible Thinking Classroom

The layout of the RTC varies from one school to the next. Most have study carrels that are usually lined up along some of the walls. The sides of the carrels extend out far enough so that each student is less inclined to look either way and see the student next to him. Regular student desks are in the middle of the room.

The teacher's desk is located near the door. In this way, any student entering the classroom is engaged quickly and efficiently so as to create as little disruption as possible to the classroom. On the corner of the desk, or on a table adjacent to the desk, are a sign-in sheet, plan sheets (see *Discipline For Home And School, Book One*, pages 59–63) and a box in which to put referral forms (*Book One*, page 116). There is also a file cabinet where all completed student plans are kept. Students are assigned numbered seats to avoid their sitting next to friends, who, for students who have just disrupted, might provide disturbances as they attempt to follow the RTC rules.

The teacher's desk is arranged to allow a view of all of the students. Often, there is a desk alongside the teacher's desk which students use when being helped with their plans. In only a few schools have we found special, enclosed rooms where the RTC teacher can work with a student while her aide monitors the classroom.

Because first-time RTC students are not familiar with the RTC, the rules of the room are often posted in large lettering for easy viewing, or there is a printed list at each desk. The rules always give directions for asking for help, asking questions, and getting permission to go to the restroom.

Sometimes a plan form is left on each desk. When students are ready to return to where they came from, they can begin working on their plans, which, when finished, they will review with the RTC teacher.

Chapter 11
What Do We Look for
When We Evaluate Schools?

W. Thomas Bourbon, Ph.D.
Perceptual Control Theorist
Rochelle, Texas

Ed Ford
RTP, Inc.
Scottsdale, Arizona

After schools use RTP for a while, they often invite us to visit and evaluate their progress. Some schools just want to know how well they are doing compared to other schools we have seen. Other schools want to know if they are doing well enough to be certified as RTP schools. In either case, before our visit, it is not unusual for someone to ask what we look for when we evaluate a school. Sometimes the best answer we can give to that question is a series of questions of our own.

Before we list some of our questions for schools, remember the following points. The essentials of RTP are spelled out in *Discipline for Home and School, Book One*. Elsewhere in this book, *Discipline for Home and School, Book Two*, are detailed descriptions of the things that happen in schools where people do RTP well—the kinds of schools that have been certified. Also in this book are descriptions of things that happen in schools where RTP is *not* done well, or where it used to be done reasonably well but staff have started to overlay it with cause-effect procedures. Keep in mind these reminders about the contents of the two books, then answer these two questions: What do you think we look for when we evaluate a school? What do you think we expect to see and hear? To answer these questions, you must be familiar with the contents of the two books—that is, with what you must know in order to do RTP well. Evaluation is as simple as that, but here are a few more questions to help you think about how well your school is using RTP.

The two most general questions we have in mind during a visit to a school are the following: Do people use *all* of the steps in the process, as described in *Book One*? Do the appropriate people fill the various roles described in *Book Two*? When we visit a school, our time is limited. We cannot be in all places in the school at one time, or in one place all of the time. We cannot see and hear everything, even in the places where we happen to be. Obviously, a visit gives us samples of what goes on in a school. The samples are limited to the places where we happen to be and the times when we are in those places. Ed spends a lot of time in the RTC, visiting with the teacher, observing how the room functions, and working on plans with students. Tom spends most of his time roaming throughout the school. Within the limitations set by the design of the school, he looks and listens for events that give the staff opportunities to use the process. He also talks to members of the staff and as many students as he can, usually outside of the classrooms, in places like the playground, the cafeteria, and the halls and walkways.

Here are examples of some specific questions that we have in mind during our visits.

1. Do teachers and other responsible people use the RTP questions at the appropriate times? When we talk to the staff about this question, we often do it in terms of "opportunities to ask the questions." During the day, did we see more opportunities taken, or more opportunities missed? You can probably imagine the range of answers to that simple question in various schools. In some schools, nearly everyone asks the appropriate questions at the appropriate times, but in others, hardly anyone does, and there are

schools where the answer might be anywhere between those two extremes. What do you think we see in schools that we certify?

When you think about each of the following questions, remember this one: What do you think we see and hear in schools that we certify?

2. Do teachers send appropriately completed referral forms when students go to the RTC?

3. Do teachers negotiate effectively and consistently when students bring plans from the RTC?

4. Does the RTP administrator understand and drive the process—does the administrator fill the role described in this book?

5. Does the RTC teacher help students create effective plans?

6. Does the RTC teacher consistently follow the process in the RTC?

7. Is the RTC a calm, quiet, and effective room?

8. Are intervention teams called promptly and in the appropriate cases?

9. Are the intervention teams effective?

10. What happens to students who make frequent visits to the RTC (the "frequent flyers")?

11. Is there evidence that people understand what RTP is about and what PCT is about? Is there evidence that people understand that RTP is not about controlling behavior —the students' or their own? Do they understand that people always try to control their own perceptions and not their behavioral actions?

12. What do students, of any age, say when we ask them questions like these: Do you know anything about RTP? What is RTP? How does it work? What do the teachers do? When do teachers ask you the RTP questions? Do all of the teachers ask the questions? What is the RTC? Do you know anyone who has been there? Do you go to the RTC for the full day? Are students punished in the RTC? Is the RTC like suspension? Is suspension better than the RTC? What do you do in the RTC? What happens after you make a plan?

What happens if a teacher doesn't like your plan? Do you have to make up work you miss while you are in the RTC? What is the RTC like—is it fun? Do you like going to the RTC? (Imagine the range of answers to the last question! For students who say they don't like the RTC but go there a lot, we ask questions like these: If you don't like the RTC, why do you keep going there? What would you need to do so you wouldn't go back? Do you think you will ever do that?) We learn a lot about how well RTP works in a school by talking with the students.

There you have it. Asking questions is a big part of what we do when we evaluate a school. Of course, we also look at any statistics and written reports that are available. *But we learn the most by looking and listening and asking simple questions.*

Chapter 12
Assessing, Evaluating, and Improving Your Commitment and Skills in RTP

George Venetis
Principal
Solano Elementary School
Osborn School District
Phoenix, Arizona

Ed Ford
RTP, Inc.
Scottsdale, Arizona

A commitment to RTP can never be simply assumed. Your present commitment depends on how much time you've taken to really understand and implement the process, including a basic understanding of perceptual control theory (PCT). This means finding out as much as possible about RTP and PCT from training, from available literature, and from those who have already successfully implemented the process. In order to self-assess where you are, the form at the end of this chapter should be helpful.

If you are committed to RTP, are clear on your role (see Chapter 8 of this book), and have identified how well you are doing, the next step is to create a plan by which you can improve your use of the process. And there is no better way to improve than by using the plan-making process used by students (see *Discipline for Home and School, Book One*, Chapter 10). But in this case, it is self-administered, with an administrator acting as guide and teacher.

The first step in making a plan for improvement is to reflect on how well you are already doing. (Note: This is not mentioned in *Book One*, Chapter 10.) Assess how you are doing by looking at areas in which you are using the process effectively. Give specific examples to support your claims. The best way to find out how well you are doing is to look at your own assessment and to find out how others perceive you using the process. Your administrator, your peers, the RTC teacher, and especially your students and their parents can give valuable insights as to how you deal with others. You could ask your students to write about how they see the process and how they think it is working. This skirts the possibility of personal attacks, yet it should reveal how your students perceive your use of RTP. This evaluation might be done after a negotiating process. Your students could be asked how well they think the process went and whether they have any questions or concerns about the entire process.

The second step is to identify an area in which you would like to improve and then establish a measurable goal which will help you evaluate how well you are progressing. Again, you should use your personal assessment and any information given to you by your students and others.

The next step is to develop a specific action plan, going into detail about how you are going to achieve your goal and specifying those from whom you are going to seek help. This is explained in *Book One*, Chapter 10.

Finally, we recommend that you select someone to use as a mentor. This person should be an experienced teacher or other staff member who understands RTP and has been using it successfully for some time. The ideal mentor is someone who is a certified RTC teacher or RTP administrator.

After you have reviewed your personal assessment form and have determined how well you use the process as perceived by others, you are now ready to complete the following plan for improving your RTP skills.

1. Based on your defined role in RTP (see Chapter 8), list two areas in which you believe you are using the process effectively. Give specific examples to support your effective

use of RTP. Refer to your assessment form where necessary.

2. Name a specific area in which would you would like to improve. The outline for the improvement section of a plan can be found on page 54 in *Book One*. As in step 1 above, you should refer to your assessment form to help identify an area for improvement.

3. Establish a measurable goal or standard by which you can know you are succeeding. This means that you should be able to establish specifically where you are now and where you want to be. The goal should be measurable in specific quantitative terms, not in vague terms. (See *Book One*, Chapter 10.)

4. Detail what you are going to do to achieve your goal (time, place, days, with whom, how long, how many, etc.). Plans must measure specifics for progress over time and specify a tool that will be used to show daily or weekly progress. This could be a check sheet, goal chart, or even periodic surveys of students, parents, or other teachers.

5. We recommend that you select as a mentor someone in whom you have a great deal of confidence—someone you respect for their integrity and experience as a seasoned teacher or administrator, who has demonstrated the correct use of the process, and who has a desire to improve his or her skills and knowledge of RTP and PCT. If possible, the person should be someone who has been certified in the process, whether as an RTC teacher or as an RTP administrator. And the person should be someone with whom you can schedule meetings to review your progress (at least once every two weeks).

The following form, although designed for teachers, can be used by anyone involved in RTP; this includes everyone who works on a school campus.

As individuals who commit to RTP continue to self-assess and self-evaluate their progress and success, their experiences in using RTP will become more satisfying.

```
              RTP/PCT SELF-ASSESSMENT FORM
```

PART I. HOW MUCH DO YOU KNOW?

(Check all items read, viewed, or attended.)

Recommended Readings:
__ Discipline For Home And School, Book One
__ Discipline For Home And School, Book Two
__ Freedom From Stress (basics of PCT)
__ Making Sense Of Behavior by W. T. Powers
   (primer on PCT)
__ Other Readings (list below)

Web page material (at www.respthink.com):
__ RTP, PCT, and Reinforcement Theory by Tom
   Bourbon
__ What Is RTP?
__ Interviews with RTP Educators
__ RTP Frequently Asked Questions by Educators
__ Results When Using RTP
__ RTP Accreditation
__ RTP and Special Education Students
__ Other Items Not Mentioned Above (list below)

Videotapes:
__ Teaching Responsible Thinking (news program
   on RTP)
__ The Heart Of The Process (understanding the
   process and theory)

Training:
___ Introductory Presentation on RTP
___ Half-Day Training with RTP Certified Person
___ Full-Day Training with Ed Ford and/or Tom Bourbon
___ Follow-Up Training with RTP Certified Person
___ Half-Day or Longer Training on PCT
___ Conference Sponsored by RTP, Inc.

School Visits:
___ Half-Day or Longer Visit to RTP Certified School
___ Half-Day or Longer Visit with RTP Certified RTC Teacher or Administrator

PART II. HOW WELL ARE YOU APPLYING RTP?

(Circle answers.)

How often are you using the questioning techniques when and where appropriate?
    All the time Most of the time Sometimes Rarely Never

Do you ask the RTP questions in a calm, curious, respectful voice?
    All the time Most of the time Sometimes Rarely Never

When a student chooses to continue to disrupt, thereby choosing to go to the RTC, do you fill out the referral form in a timely fashion?
    All the time Most of the time Sometimes Rarely Never

After filling out the referral form, how often do you get further requests to explain what happened?

    All the time Most of the time Sometimes
    Rarely Never

When you negotiate with the student prior to his/her re-entering your class:

A. Do you meet at your earliest convenience?
    Always Sometimes Never

B. Do you listen to his/her explanations?
    Always Sometimes Never

C. Do you suggest alternatives to his/her plan to help the student succeed?
    Always Sometimes Never

D. Do you suggest future meetings to review the student's progress?
    Always Sometimes Never

How often do you hold classroom discussions (see Book One, Chapter 6, page 23)?

    Daily More than once a week Once a week
    Seldom Never

When you have concerns, how often do you talk with the RTC teacher?

    Every time Most of the time Sometimes
    Rarely Never

When you have concerns, how often do you talk with your administrator?

    Every time Most of the time Sometimes
    Rarely Never

When you have concerns, how often do you talk
with anyone other than your administrator or the
RTC teacher?
   Every time Most of the time Sometimes
   Rarely Never

Have you ever recommended an intervention team
meeting to discuss a particular student?
   Yes, when needed Yes, once Never

When you communicate with parents concerning
the various aspects of RTP:
A. Have you made sure that they understand the
process?   Yes No

B. Have you answered any questions about RTP?
   Yes No

C. Have you suggested available reading
materials?   Yes No

D. Have you given them the RTP card?   Yes No

E. Have you suggested and explained a homework
plan for their child?   Yes No

List any other areas not included above that you
feel are necessary to your self-evaluation.

Chapter 13
Are You Living Your Commitment?

LeEdna Custer-Knight
School Psychologist
Clarendon Elementary School
Osborn School District
Phoenix, Arizona

Commitment

Commitment is what transforms a promise into reality.
It is the words that speak boldly of your intentions,
And the actions which speak louder than the words.
It is making the time when there is none,
Coming through time after time, year after year.
Commitment is the stuff character is made of,
The power to change the face of things.
It is the daily triumph of integrity over skepticism.

This anonymous poem hangs on the wall of my office and daily reminds me that commitment is no small thing. It is a word often used for effect or impact. We have commitment statements, are committed to a project, philosophy, whatever. We even claim to be in "committed" relationships. True commitment is not something you talk about, it is something you live. Ed and George have spent considerable time attempting to provide an instrument (in Chapter 12) to be used as a guide for self-evaluation of commitment and progress in the Responsible Thinking Process. Theirs is a laudable effort and for many will provide a structure through which they can screen their actions to gain insight into their levels of alignment with their stated goals in the process. But I am leery of checklists and evaluation instruments because too often I have found people utilizing them not as intended (i.e., broad markers of alignment), but rather as points of compliance to be quickly and efficiently checked off as absolute evidence of success.

Meeting the criteria might become more important than developing a conceptual understanding of perceptual control theory and the Responsible Thinking Process. However, the only true means of sustaining alignment is through conceptual understanding.

Perceptual control theory, which is the theoretical basis of the Responsible Thinking Process, presents a radical shift in our view of man. Historically, behavioral scientists have viewed man as a victim of his environment. Popular interpretation of these theories has led many to believe individuals can be controlled by means of conditioning and reinforcement. This has been particularly true of teacher training and most popular parenting programs. Teachers have been taught that they can control student behavior and are routinely held responsible for the behavior of children in their classes. Parents are also taught that they can easily control their children's behavior by systematically applying the use of reinforcers and/or conditioning. Since the 1960s, we have seen the prolific propagation of charts, stickers, tokens, and point systems, all for the expressed purpose of controlling children by modifying their behavior. In these programs, children are seen as passive subjects to whom the programs are applied. This well-entrenched behavioristic view of man as controlled by his environment is still pervasive in our society. It is the means by which schools and parents attempt to control our children, the military our servicemen and women, and the prisons their inmates.

Commitment to the Responsible Thinking Process requires an incredible shift in belief systems. It requires that we abandon the illusion of control of others and embrace the concept of man as a living control system. To make that shift at a systems concept level requires significant re-education and effort. It requires a significant change in the way we live. Therein lies my concern with Ed and George's markers of alignment. If utilized as intended, they become meaningful; however, if used as markers to be checked off, participation in the Responsible Thinking Process becomes yet another quick-fix recipe for dealing with discipline. Time and again, I have seen individuals commit to the process, learn the RTP questioning techniques, utilize the responsible thinking classroom, negotiate with students, and then state that they understand the Responsible Thinking Process. Later, I have seen the same people engaged in the use of reinforcers, punishment, and "telling" children what they must do, with no apparent awareness that these acts are in complete conflict with the process and the view of man as a living control system.

The first indicator that you might be slipping away conceptually is if you perceive commitment to the Responsible Thinking Process as an easy shift. The second might be that you have no sense of profound and global change in the dynamics of your relationships with others. For me, there has been a profound increase in my respect for the perceptions of others. I accept that individuals' perceptions are their only reality and that their behaviors are their attempts to correct perceptual errors and align their reality with the ways they want to perceive the world. Commitment means the abandonment of judgment as to the meaning of observed behaviors or actions. Perhaps the most difficult change required is the abandonment of the illusion of control. Implicit in every aspect of our culture, and inherent in our hierarchical systems of management, is the belief that rewards and punishments can effectively control individuals. To assert that it is an easy transition to abandon what for most is a lifetime of implicit and explicit education in cause-effect psychology is reason for concern. There is little in our current society that does not, at some level, have an underpinning of behavioristic stimulus-response theory. It is there in the "telling" of children, students, and employees. It is there in the pats on the back and the stickers and bonuses for jobs well done. It is there in the spanking, yelling, and reprimands for failure to behave as directed. It can be overwhelmingly explicit, as in behavior management programs or levels systems in prisons and treatment centers. Often it is implicit, as in family dynamics and corporate structures. In our society, those individuals who become adept at recognizing the stimulus as a performance cue and are quick to perform the desired behavior are viewed favorably.

Commitment to the Responsible Thinking Process requires that we carefully screen not only our formal processes but also the underlying culture of our organization and our lives for evidence of coercion, reinforcement, and punishment. This is not a simple task, nor is it a singular event. We must continually revisit our practices to determine ongoing alignment with our theoretical basis. Commitment to the Responsible Thinking Process means changing the way we choose to live with one another. It means acknowledging the fact that an individual's behaviors control his or her perceptions. Organizationally, it is the commitment to the development of a community vision of how all members want to perceive their experiences together. In schools, this is probably best achieved by classroom discussions about what an ideal school or class would look like, sound like, and feel like. Out of these discussions would be generated a consensus of standards that all can agree to live by, and a plan for dealing with conflict or unintended consequences of acting to achieve goals. At no time in this process is it appropriate to dictate group standards —it won't work if we do. To continue to maximize the opportunity for long-term success in this process requires frequent dialogue among all members as to their perceptions of their experiences in the organization. It requires ongoing dedication to eliminate all vestiges of behaviorism from the environment. But most importantly, it requires systematic change in our most basic understanding of how all life is organized.

To relegate determination of your adherence to this process to something as simple as markers fails to acknowl-

edge acceptance of perceptual control theory as a profoundly life-changing event.

Chapter 14
The Intervention Team:
Jewel in the Crown of RTP

Timothy A. Carey
Certified RTP Trainer and Evaluator
Brisbane, Queensland, Australia

Margaret Carey
Certified RTC Teacher
Minimbah State School
Morayfield, Queensland, Australia

Intervention teams (see *Discipline for Home and School, Book One*, pages 70–72, and *Book Two*, pages 41–42) are an enigmatic aspect of the Responsible Thinking Process. When a school first implements RTP, the formation and functioning of intervention teams is typically given a low priority. This is understandable in the early stages of coming to terms with a new approach to discipline, but intervention teams must eventually become a central element of the process. Intervention teams are so important that their success is one of the principal defining features of well-functioning RTP schools.

In this chapter, we outline what intervention teams are and why they are important, and we suggest a format for intervention team meetings. Schools that are seriously considering implementation of RTP must give some time to understanding the role that intervention teams play in the process. To help illustrate the ideas and suggestions being discussed, several examples are included, based on experiences at Minimbah State School.

About this Chapter

Throughout this chapter and particularly throughout the form at the end of this chapter, you might come across terms that are unfamiliar. This has been done intentionally as an attempt to introduce you to some of the concepts of perceptual control theory. We believe that a good understanding of PCT by school staff is particularly important when dealing with the small percentage of students for whom intervention teams are convened. Conventional interventions in schools, whether they advocate dispensing punishments and rewards or satisfying student needs, all seem to have the common goal of changing student behavior. But some students have frustrated all such attempts to manage their behavior. It is for these students that knowledge of PCT is crucial. Fundamentally, PCT requires an answer to the question, "Am I willing to give up the idea that I can make other people do what I want them to do?" The "difficult" students are generally those who are exposed to more attempts by staff to control them and have more done *to* them than other students. It is time for a change. PCT allows that change to be made.

This is the motivation for the construction of this chapter. The use of PCT terminology is not meant to frighten or intimidate readers. This chapter is meant to provide you with an opportunity to learn more about PCT in order to help all students experience success at school. If some terms and concepts in this chapter seem confusing, it might be helpful to refer back to Chapters 2 and 31 of *Book One*, where PCT ideas are introduced. Knowledge of PCT will help you make more sense of interactions occurring in your school, so you might want to learn more. This chapter is an attempt to help you do so.

What Is an Intervention Team?

Most students experience benefits from RTP soon after the process is introduced. The majority of students in a school implementing RTP will experience increased academic learning time, reduced interpersonal conflict, and more opportunities to learn to solve problems in socially appropriate ways. However, for a small but significant percentage of the student population (usually between two and five percent), these benefits take much longer to be experienced. Typically, such students are experiencing major difficulties in their lives and need additional support in order to succeed in school. The intervention team process is designed to investigate ways for this additional support to be offered to these students.

Whenever a student experiences ongoing difficulty in school, an intervention team meeting should be convened. If a student has made three or more plans in a week, or if a student sits in class for more than a day or two and does no work at all but does not disrupt either, or if a student sits in the responsible thinking classroom for more than a full day and has not made a plan to get back to the area he or she disrupted in, or if a student has gone home and has not returned to school within a day or two, an intervention team meeting is appropriate.

The intervention team is different from other school teams and committees in that it is not made up of the same people each time it meets, and it does not convene at a regularly appointed time. The individuals involved in a particular intervention team depend on the student for whom the meeting has been called. On every team will be the RTP administrator and the RTC teacher; also on the team will be the teacher (or staff member) from the area where the student disrupted, the student's parent(s) or guardian(s) (if possible), and others who might have important information about the student (such as guidance counselors, psychologists, behavior intervention specialists, tutors, learning support teachers, and other employees of the school). While the parent(s) or guardian(s) should be thought of as important members of the team, if for some reason they are not able to be part of the team, the team should still meet. A meeting should never be postponed because parent(s) or guardian(s) have difficulty attending. The student is not present at this meeting, although he or she may nominate for the team a staff member in the school with whom he or she has a special relationship, such as his or her home room teacher or sports coach.

When determining who should be part of the intervention team, it is important to consider school staff who will have something to contribute regarding the student. For example, Lachlan is a 10-year-old boy who, some months ago, made frequent trips to the RTC for disrupting in class. An intervention team meeting was convened, and it was suggested that Lachlan had a hearing problem that could be contributing to his difficulties. Subsequently, Lachlan's mother had his hearing assessed; it was determined that he had significant hearing loss in one ear. Once Lachlan's hearing loss was compensated for, he was able to succeed in class and made no further visits to the RTC. The reason this intervention team decided to investigate Lachlan's hearing was because of people on the team. Lachlan's mother mentioned that he had had an ear infection some time ago, Lachlan's teacher noticed that Lachlan seemed to have attentional difficulties when sitting in particular positions in the room, and the guidance counselor, who had a background in special education, suggested that a hearing problem might be a possibility. In Lachlan's case, then, if any of these people had not been on the team, his hearing problems might not have been detected.

The convening of an intervention team could occur through the core team. The nature of the core team is described in Chapter 13 of *Book One*. Essentially, a core team of people, including the administrator, the RTC teacher, the guidance counselor, interested teachers, a parent representative, and a student representative meet regularly (e.g., weekly) to discuss the operation of RTP. These meetings provide an ideal time to discuss any forthcoming intervention team meetings. The core team could discuss any information that should be gathered before the intervention team convenes, and also who would be part of this particular intervention team. The core team could also assign responsibility for the coordination of the intervention team to a staff member.

In many instances, the guidance counselor in the school is an ideal person to coordinate the intervention team meeting. The person who takes on this responsibility should have a good knowledge of both RTP and PCT. The person who coordinates the intervention team meeting should briefly report the results of the meeting back to the core team.

Why Are Intervention Teams Necessary?

One of the principles of perceptual control theory (see *Book One*, Chapters 2 and 31, and *Book Two*, Chapter 7), upon which RTP is based, is that people develop goals and expectations about the world based on the ways they experience the world. Because of their prior experiences, some students come into schools with expectations and goals about themselves and others that make it exceedingly difficult for them to succeed. Some might believe, for example, that if they want something that someone else has, they can just take it. Some might expect adults to criticize and ridicule them. And some might believe that no one will like them. Also, some students develop such expectations and goals while at school. Some students experience school as a place where they are constantly told what to do, or where they are punished or criticized. Or they might experience school as a place where they fail at many things. These students sometimes develop goals for avoiding people or situations where they fail, and they might learn clever ways to be left alone. Thus, for a variety of reasons, a few students in every school find it very difficult to achieve goals that are important to them without preventing other people from achieving their own goals.

The cornerstone of RTP is to maintain an invitational attitude while offering students opportunities to succeed. Just as students who experience academic difficulties are offered extra support in order to learn what they need to learn, so too students who experience social difficulties are offered extra support in order to learn how to get along with others. And just as academic support is continually offered to students regardless of how quickly or slowly the work is learned, so too the RTP invitation to succeed is continually offered to students experiencing social difficulties. There is no time limit in RTP.

The purpose of the intervention team, then, is to decide on an appropriate level of support that will be offered to the unsuccessful student, so that he or she might experience school differently and begin to succeed. It is *not* the purpose of the intervention team to make decisions about what can be *done to* the student so that he or she might spend more time in class. When a student begins to visit the RTC regularly, the notion must be entertained that the student might be intentionally using the RTC to control some of his or her experiences at school. To try to stop the student from using the RTC in this way, without some understanding of what might be going on for the student, is a sure way to lay the foundations for counter-control (see *Book Two*, pages 33–34) and conflict. Counter-control is the situation that can occur whenever one person specifies how another person must act. Therefore, any time a teacher decides how the students in her class must act, counter-control is likely. Whenever a teacher experiences frustration or annoyance at how the students in her class are acting, it is likely that counter-control is occurring.

Schools where time is devoted in intervention team meetings to deciding on the support to be offered to students are generally schools where staff have a solid understanding of both RTP and PCT. These schools typically enjoy much success with RTP. Other schools in which intervention team members use their meetings to decide what to *do to* students, or perhaps even to decide that particular students are "outside" the process, are schools in which the fundamental principles of RTP and PCT are not really understood. Before long, the discipline process in these latter schools begins to resemble programs based on traditional theories of psychology (see *Book One*, page 239). The intervention team determines the types of support to be offered to the student. The intervention team does *not* make decisions about how the student should act. Spending time specifying how the student should act is a sure way of establishing a counter-control situation.

Conducting an Intervention Team Meeting

At the end of this chapter is a form that we have found useful when beginning to implement an intervention team process. This form need not be rigidly followed. Rather, it should be treated as one way to gather and organize information coming out of an intervention team meeting. Each section of the form is discussed separately below. Some of what is presented below might be unfamiliar to you. You are invited to begin with what is comfortable for you.

Relationships

The kinds of one-on-one relationships that students have with significant adults are an important consideration. Quality time is an experience between two people that Ed Ford has described in detail in *Book One* and *Freedom from Stress*. It is vital for students who are experiencing chronic difficulties at school to begin spending time with an adult in enjoyable, constructive activities. Such experiences give students opportunities to think of themselves as being valued and appreciated. Through these experiences, students might learn to appreciate the importance of qualities such as trust, respect, and cooperation. Classroom discussions are one way of providing valuable social experiences for groups of students. However, such discussions should not be viewed as substitutes for one-on-one quality-time experiences, but rather as supplements to quality-time experiences between a student and an adult. Nothing is so important as having quality time with another human being. Classroom discussions are outlined by Le Edna

Custer-Knight in *Book One*, Chapter 24.

During the intervention team meeting, inquiries should be made about quality time at home, as an opportunity to teach the student's parent(s) or guardian(s) about the concept of quality time if they are interested. However, these inquiries should never be used to try to make the parent(s) or guardian(s) accountable for the student's behavior. The invitational attitude that is so much a part of RTP extends to the parent(s)/guardian(s) as well as to the student.

At a recent Minimbah intervention team meeting, it was determined that six-year-old Eloise had very disjointed relationships in her life. At home, there was only one parent; because of work commitments, the parent was unable to spend much time with Eloise. At school, Eloise found it very difficult to establish a satisfying relationship with anyone. The recommendation of the meeting was that a teacher's aide should spend time each day working with Eloise, establishing a relationship with her. After this simple strategy was implemented, people noticed a major change in the way Eloise functioned at school. She began to build better relationships with people and also began to improve in her school work.

Using the Process

It is vital that the intervention team should spend time investigating whether or not RTP is being used as well as it can be with the student. There might be some instances where the process is not being used at all. The RTP questions might not have been asked, or perhaps the negotiation process did not occur with this student. There is little point in spending a school's precious time and resources when a student's difficulties might be addressed by simply following the process. If the process is not being followed, then this should be the first correction to be made before any more elaborate support is offered. The reference to the home in this section of the form is included as an opportunity to provide parents with information about the process if they are interested in learning about it.

Use of the process might be improved in a number of ways. Perhaps the teacher is asking the RTP questions in an attempt to control the actions of the student. The problem then might be no more than a counter-control situation. Or perhaps the student is not really committed to his plan, so that other people are doing most of the work to make the plan succeed. In this case, questions should be asked of the student that specifically address how important the plan is *to the student*. Questions such as: "On a scale of 1 to 10, how serious are you about this plan?"; "How important is it to you to be back in class?"; "What are you making this plan for?"; "What will being back in class help you achieve?"; and "Are you sure you want to be back in class?" might give some clues as to whether or not the student is making a serious attempt to make the plan work.

Miss Middleton decided during an intervention team meeting that she would conduct classroom discussions with her class, because Andrew, the student for whom the meeting was being conducted, had significant problems playing with other students. During the classroom discussions, Miss Middleton was able to invite students to discuss various aspects of playing with each other. These discussions also gave Andrew the opportunity to talk about the problems he had when attempting to play with others. The teacher observed an improvement in her whole class generally, and Andrew specifically, in the ways they interacted with each other.

Controlled Variables

In PCT, it is recognized that human beings live in an environment that constantly varies. To a large degree, this variation goes unnoticed because we are so good at making the environment vary in the ways we want. Think for a moment of all of the variations that are possible in a classroom. If you were a silent observer in a classroom, even for a short time, what would you observe? The noise level might vary, the positions of the students and the teacher might vary, the amount of work being produced might vary, the temperature might vary, the number of people in the room might vary, etc. What we find, though, when we observe environments with people in them, is that, by and large, much of the variation that we might expect *doesn't* occur. In a classroom, for example, noise level tends to stay fairly constant. This is not to say that noise level doesn't change at all, rather that it changes much less than we might otherwise expect. Variations are possible everywhere. Imagine the variations that are possible while you are driving your car. The speed of the car can vary; so can its position in the road. What we find when we observe people driving cars, however, is that these variable aspects of driving tend to change very little, and, when they do change, they change in *systematic* ways.

The ability of living things to prevent aspects of their environment from changing or to make these aspects change in systematic ways is essentially what PCT is explaining. In PCT, things that can change or vary are called *variables*. When a variable is prevented from varying, it is said to be controlled. In PCT, it is acknowledged that people do *not* control "things," but they do control variable *aspects* of those things, which are experienced by them. When I drive my car, for example, I don't control my car, but I try to control the speed of my car and the position of the car in the road as I experience those variables. In a classroom, teachers don't control "students," but they might try to control the noise level they hear from the students, the amount of work they see the students producing, or the direction they see the students facing.

In Chapter 2 of *Book One*, Ed Ford describes a classroom situation. In this example, we can see that Hunter had something on his mind. The thing on Hunter's mind at the time was the amount of attention he was receiving from Sally Ann. Obviously, attention can vary from "none" to "constant," so we can think of attention as a variable. In this example, Hunter didn't want Sally Ann's attention to vary in just *any* way; he wanted it to vary in a *particular* way. Thus, we can say that Hunter was trying to *control* the amount of attention he received from Sally Ann. From a PCT perspective, Sally Ann's attention was a controlled variable for Hunter. Similarly, Mrs. Johnson was concerned about the level of noise in the room. Because noise can vary from "silent" to "very loud," we can call the room noise a variable. Because Mrs. Johnson wanted to hear a *particular* level of noise, and because she *acted* in certain ways so as to hear the particular level of noise that she wanted to hear, we can say that the room noise level was a controlled variable for Mrs. Johnson.

To help students make successful plans, it is important to have some idea of what they are controlling for. Understanding what a person is controlling for in terms of controlled variables (see *Book One*, page 230) is a key feature of perceptual control theory. Such control does not occur haphazardly; rather, it occurs *with reference to* particular values. The particular value of a controlled variable that a person wants is known theoretically as a *reference perception*, but it can also be thought of as a want, goal, intention, expectation, or desire. It is important to note that a person's reference perception for a controlled variable (e.g., room noise level) can be different under different conditions (e.g., a test vs. a discussion).

It is *not* possible to observe the reference perceptions of a student in terms of the goals, standards, expectations, or specifications that the student might want. It *is* possible, however, to observe the environment in which the student functions. In this environment are variables that the student wants to perceive as being in particular states. By manipulating the environment that you share with the student, and by astute observation, it is possible to gain some sense of the way in which the student wants to experience the environment. This also can be done conversationally by discussing with the student how he or she is experiencing the environment, and what he or she might do upon sensing changes in the environment.

A conversation to investigate what a student who yells out in class might be controlling for could go something like this:

Mr. Smith: What happens when you yell in class?

Preston: I get asked some questions.

Mr. Smith: And then what happens?

Preston: I yell again, and then I go to the RTC.

Mr. Smith: What is usually happening at the time you are yelling out?

Preston: I'm doing work in class.

Mr. Smith: Do you like doing class work?

Preston: Some.

Mr. Smith: What work do you like?

Preston: I like math.

Mr. Smith: What is it that you like about math?

Preston: It's easy, and I get it all right.

Mr. Smith: Do you ever yell out in math?

Preston: Nope. I like math.

Mr. Smith: When do you usually yell out?

Preston: I yell out in reading and spelling.

Mr. Smith: Do you find reading and spelling easy?

Preston: No. They're really hard.

Mr. Smith: What happens to the reading and spelling that you miss out on when you're in the RTC?

Preston: I have to do it for homework.

Mr. Smith: Is it easier to do it at home?

Preston: Yep, because I have lots of time, and my sister helps me.

Mr. Smith: If you had someone to help you at school, and you had lots of time, would it be easy?

Preston: Sure would.

Mr. Smith: Would you still yell out in spelling and reading if you found them easy?

Preston: No way.

From this conversation, Mr. Smith now has an idea that Preston is controlling a variable that has to do with the degree of difficulty Preston perceives in his work. When the controlled variables are revealed, the student's actions sud-

denly make sense. Yelling out during spelling and reading
is Preston's way of reducing the degree of difficulty of the
work to the level he wants it to be. A student's actions
become much more meaningful to school staff when they
are related to presumed controlled variables, allowing a
concrete plan to be recommended. Mr. Smith might have
originally had many ideas about why Preston was yelling
out. For example, Preston might have been yelling out to
get the teacher to notice him, or he might have been yelling out so that other students would laugh and then he
would feel approved of by his peers. In this instance, however, if Mr. Smith had helped Preston make a plan for getting his teacher's attention or for getting peer approval in
non-disruptive ways, this plan would have had very little
chance of succeeding. It is only when plans address the
variables that are important to the student that they are likely to be successful.

Hamish visited the RTC frequently because of hitting
other students in the playground. Some of the teachers felt
that Hamish was bullying other students in an attempt to
frighten and intimidate them. By focusing on what Hamish
was controlling for, however, it was determined that he was
trying to play with the other students. He actually liked the
other students and just wanted them to play with him.
When they wanted to play something else, Hamish didn't
know how to communicate with them to get what he wanted. Knowledge of what Hamish was likely to be controlling
for had important implications for the plan that he would
make. A plan to improve Hamish's communication abilities
would be much more meaningful to Hamish than a plan
that addressed issues having to do with frightening and
intimidating other students.

This part of the form also provides an opportunity to
determine whether or not the student's problems might be
due to a difficulty in controlling certain perceptions. Perhaps the student's difficulties result from a lack of skill in
doing what is required. If this is the case, the student might
need to learn certain things. How this might be accom-

plished is covered in the next section. Also, the student's difficulties might result from conflict that the student is experiencing. For example, the student might want a high level of approval from peers and a low level of difficulty with the teacher. However, doing things to stay out of trouble with the teacher might result in teasing from the other students. Then the student will act to reduce the amount of teasing. However, these actions might then get the student in trouble with the teacher. This situation poses a dilemma for the student, who will need support to develop a plan to achieve both peer approval and minimal difficulties with the teacher. Finally, the student's problems might be the result of insuperable disturbances. These are forces in the environment that are just too great to oppose. The student, for example, might be using the RTC in lunch breaks because of a threatening gang of other students. Unable to work out this problem with the gang, the student retreats to the RTC to stay safe.

Deficits in Learning

According to PCT, what we learn are control systems. We do not learn skills, or actions, or responses, but we learn instead to control perceived variables. It might be the case that the intervention team determines that the student has never learned to control a particular variable. If students have come from particularly abusive home environments, for example, where they are criticized and ridiculed and constantly told what to do, they might never have experienced cooperation. It makes no sense at all, then, to expect these students to control for variables related to cooperation. In this instance, intervention teams might decide that it is important to provide such students with opportunities to learn to control for cooperative experiences.

Someone working with such a student might first provide the student with lots of experiences of cooperation. Quality time would be a perfect context for this. Then the person could spend time with the student, asking about different amounts of cooperation ("When was a time when someone cooperated with you a lot?"; "When were some times when people didn't cooperate with you at all, or not very much?"). Next, the student could be encouraged to think about the amount of cooperation he or she would like to experience ("How much cooperation would you like to have?") and to explore the consequences of this level of cooperation ("What will be the best part of this amount of cooperation?"; "What problems might there be in this amount of cooperation?"; "What might other people think if you cooperate this much?"; "What will the consequences for you be if people think of you in that way?"). After this, the student could be encouraged to identify times when he or she is not experiencing the amount of cooperation he or she wants to experience. This can be done conversationally ("If 'this' happened, would that be the amount of cooperation you would want?"), or experientially ("At this very moment, are you getting the amount of cooperation you want?"). When the amount of cooperation the student wants to experience is different from the amount of cooperation the student is actually experiencing, the student should be encouraged to explore ways of reducing the difference ("How will you make cooperation be the way you want it to be?"; "What will happen if you do that?"; "Is that what you want?"; "What else could you do?"). Finally, the student needs many opportunities to practice controlling for this variable across a range of settings. This practice could be facilitated through quality time and also by the use of plans and feedback charts.

Recommendations

The final section in the form provides room for the team participants to summarize the outcomes of the meeting with regard to the level of support the team will offer the student, so that the student might begin to experience success at school. Also, spaces are provided to specify who will take responsibility for working with the student and to specify a time when the team will reconvene to evaluate how helpful the current level of support has been for the student. There is also space for team participants to sign the form.

Concluding Remarks

Creative and efficient intervention teams convene when a student experiences chronic difficulties at school, focus on what the student might be controlling for, and determine what level of support the school might be able to offer the student to help him or her succeed. Such intervention teams are perhaps *the* hallmark of an outstanding RTP school. It is the intervention team aspect of RTP that, more than any other single element of the process, offers real hope to the most difficult students. It is through the intervention team process that these students can learn to experience success at school, and, through that success, can learn to function as successful adults in society. The success or failure of intervention teams hinges entirely on the attitudes of their members. Attitudes focusing on what can be done to students to increase desirable behavior and to decrease undesirable behavior are no different from the attitudes that underpin other discipline programs. The results, therefore, can be expected to be no different. Different results begin with a different attitude, and it is the attitude of invitation and offering support, based on the principles of PCT, that makes all the difference.

GUIDELINES FOR INTERVENTION TEAM MEETINGS

Date:
Student:
Intervention Team Members (Names & Positions):

Number of plans made by student to date:
Number of previous intervention team meetings:
Action from last intervention team meeting:

Results of this action:

What aspects of the support provided did the
student find helpful?

What aspects of the support provided need to be
changed or modified?

RELATIONSHIPS:
Does the student spend quality time with anyone?
    At home: yes   no
    At school: yes   no
If yes, who does he/she spend time with, how
much time, and what are the activities?

Do any changes need to be made with the student's
involvement in quality time?   yes   no
If so, what changes need to be made?

Does the student participate in classroom
discussions?   never   occasionally
                average   quite a bit

USING THE PROCESS:
Is the student asked the RTP questions
consistently?
    At home: yes   no
    At school: yes   no
Do any changes need to be made with the asking
of the RTP questions?   yes   no
If yes, what changes need to be made?

Does the student have a specific goal to work on in his/her plan?   yes   no
Does the student have a feedback chart?
    yes   no
Have possible disturbances been anticipated in the student's plan?   yes   no
Who are the people involved with him/her in his/her plan?

Are they cooperative?
    never   rarely   half the time   always
How much time is currently being devoted to negotiating the plan between the student and the teacher?
Who would the student say is most responsible for the success of this plan?
    the student   others
Do any changes to the planning process need to be made with this student?   yes   no
If yes, what changes need to be made?

CONTROLLED VARIABLES:
What might the student possibly be controlling for?

What evidence is there for this hypothesized controlled variable?

What reference level do you think the student
has for the variable that is being controlled?

What evidence is there for this reference level?

Is the student experiencing difficulties
controlling perceptions that are important in
terms of: lack of skill   conflict
               insuperable disturbances
Comments:

DEFICITS IN LEARNING:
Does this student need to learn to control a
specific variable in order to function
successfully in a social group?   yes no
What variable does the student need to learn to
control?

Is the student able to perceive this variable?
    yes no need to determine
Has the student experienced different states of
this variable?   yes no need to determine
Can the student remember different states of
this variable?   yes no need to determine
Does the student have a preferred state for this
variable?   yes no need to determine

Is the student able to differentiate between the
preferred state and other states of the
variable?   yes no need to determine
When the student experiences this variable in
states other than the one he prefers, is he able
to describe how he would change the variable
from its current state back to the preferred
state?   yes no need to determine
Has the student had adequate opportunities to
practice keeping this variable in its preferred
state across a range of different settings?
      yes no need to determine
What opportunities need to be provided to this
student to help him/her learn to control this
variable?

Have any of the above questions in this section
been a part of the student's plan making in the
past?   yes no
If yes, what has been fully successful,
partially successful, and not successful?

RECOMMENDATIONS:
What action does the intervention team now
recommend to help this student succeed?

Who will take responsibility for working with this student?

When will the intervention team meet again?

SIGNED (Signature & Printed Name/Position):

Part 3. Advice from Some Who Are Using RTP

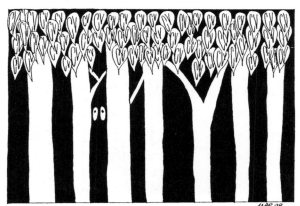

SOMETIMES WE CAN'T SEE THE CVs FOR THE FOREST ... WORKING WITH FREQUENT FLYERS!!

SOMETIMES WHAT PEOPLE ARE CONTROLLING FOR (CVs) IS NOT ALWAYS OBVIOUS. INTERVENTION TEAMS PROVIDE AN OPPORTUNITY FOR EXPLORATION!!

Chapter 15
Comments by Educators
Who Are Implementing RTP

Establishing the
Responsible Thinking Process
Is a Continuum

Steve Smith
Principal
Boyne City Middle School
Boyne City, Michigan

We began our implementation of RTP by having all staff members receive two days of inservice from Ed Ford during August. Then we spent the next four months building procedures and learning more about perceptual control theory. By December, we had staff buy-in, a set of goals, our procedures, and support from the district to hire personnel to run the RTC. In January, we were off and running! Everything would go smoothly from this point forward—or so we thought.

While we saw lots of things that we liked, questions began to arise. For example: "What do you mean, I can't send him to the RTC for sitting in class and not doing anything?" This became an issue about which some staff members struggled. Our surveys found people at both ends of the issue. Some were looking for a quick fix and would send students to the RTC whenever they were not following instructions. Others struggled with having students out of their classrooms. They felt it was their job to work with the students, who, if gone, would miss too much. As a result, we needed to take a step back and look at a couple of issues. First, we looked at the goals we had established for the process. What we had agreed to was to protect the teaching and learning environment from disrespect and disruptions. We had put this process in place to help us teach the students self-discipline. Was not doing work a disruption? While we agreed it was a concern, we talked about the other types of interventions we had in place to address this issue and agreed to separate the two situations. Second, we reviewed the concept of what it means to protect the teaching and learning environment. Was taking class time to work with a student lessening the time we had to teach other students? Was standing in the hall, with one eye and ear on the room, sending the message we wanted to the disrupting student? Were we really helping these students to become responsible thinkers? These questions led us to more reading, inservice, and discussion. Eventually, we began to see that we needed to be consistent, and that if we wanted students to learn to be thinkers, we had to teach them. We also saw how working with students could be more effective during the negotiation part of the process. We really were not giving up a part of our job but doing it with more quality time.

But what about the "frequent flyers" (an affectionate name for those who often visit the RTC)? Don't we need to up the stakes if, after several visits, they don't "come around"? The issue for us related to the belief system that we all had experience with: cause-effect—just up the consequences or do more to them, and they will come around. Most of us can look back and find examples where doing more to "control" others appeared to work. And in some cases, especially with compliant students, at least in the short term, it did appear to get us what we wanted. But is that what we *really* want? Or do we want students who are accountable for their actions, able to resolve problems in a calm and respectful manner, and learning to be responsible thinkers? In math, for example, we know that students are at different points in their learning, and they learn at different rates. Therefore, we asked whether this was also true for learning how to solve issues related to disruptions. Also, if doing more to them is not the answer, then what else can we do?

Fortunately, the frequent flyers tend to be less than five percent of any school's population. For these students, the answer seems to be consistency, understanding that this is a teaching process, and providing opportunities for quality time with significant adults. What we have begun to realize is that the key person is the RTC teacher, who sees the big picture regarding frequent flyers. When she notices a person struggling, she "throws the switch," and administratively we put an intervention team in place. This allows several adults to take active roles in working with a student. This is a continuous process, which means that everyone who interacts with the students can help teach and model for the students how to think for themselves and successfully solve their problems through plan making. It is the RTC teacher who plays a major role in teaching plan making and working closely with staff to assist in its implementation. Also, we saw that the negotiation portion of the process could be used to enhance quality time. For success to occur with these students, they first must perceive that staff members care about them. Spending time one-on-one with these students can lead to stronger relationships.

We are now in our fifth year using RTP. It has not always been easy, but it is evolving into a successful process. Indicators that we are getting there can be seen in the following stories.

A staff member came into our team meeting and stated, "This is really great! It is working! For negotiations, I took Susie out of class, and we went for a walk outside to work on her plan. A half hour later, when we came back in, I noticed a smile on her face which I had seldom seen. And better yet, she has continued to be upbeat and display that smile for the past several days."

Another staff member came into my office and in the process of our conversation stated, "This past summer I had an interview, not that I was really thinking of moving, and after it was over and I was discussing it with my wife, I realized that I had a dilemma. There was something really different about the climate in that school. I wasn't comfortable with the general feeling of how they worked with each other. As a result, it would be very hard for me to move to a district that doesn't believe in RTP. I don't think I could be successful in that environment, and I know I couldn't go back to the old way of doing business."

Recently, we have been doing some research into new math programs. As part of our study, several staff members have been visiting other schools. A couple of interesting comments have been shared by one of our teachers. He said, "Boy, it was really hard to sit there. I just wanted to get up and go ask, 'What are you doing? What are the rules?' I could see that the disruptions and the way the teacher was dealing with them were keeping a high-quality lesson from being successful." He also shared that he could now see another benefit of RTP: "I know it has taken us a while to get to where we are today. But after sitting in several of those classes, it's very obvious to me how RTP also helps students become better thinkers and problem solvers, and will allow us to successfully implement a more constructivist or inquiry mode of teaching."

As the stories show, we are becoming the school we envisioned we could be. Remember though, it is a process, and as a process, it is always ongoing. Be committed, but be patient. We each enter new experiences with our own perceptions, and therefore it takes a while to bring our various beliefs together. Work through the issues to help each other as a team. Be understanding of the differences and realize that we begin at different places on the continuum just like our students in any given learning situation. The time and energy are well worth it, because when it becomes a way of life in a school, it establishes an environment where everyone can be successful.

The Counselor's Role in RTP

Harriet H. West
Counselor
Casa Blanca Community School
Gila River Indian Reservation
Bapchule, Arizona

During the past three years, I have been very fortunate to work in a school that has implemented the Responsible Thinking Process. RTP has made a tremendous difference in helping our students become more responsible for how they deal with others.

Among educators, there is much discussion about how essential it is for parents to become involved with their children's schools. RTP provides parents with many opportunities to work cooperatively with school staff. When we have intervention team meetings, parents begin to see the total picture of what choices their children are making at school. No longer do they blame staff for not doing enough for their children. Requiring parents to attend intervention team meetings communicates to them that they are part of a team helping their children make better choices at school.

At intervention team meetings, I, as counselor, help unite the school staff's concerns with the parents' concerns. It is difficult for some parents to accept feedback about their children. They sometimes take it as a personal attack on their parenting skills rather than as a report on their children's poor choices. On several occasions, my role has been to support parents' efforts to cooperate with the school staff by urging them to attend intervention team meetings in a timely manner. They most certainly need to be encouraged to feel comfortable and to understand that we are trying to establish cooperative and supportive relationships. Some parents who at first seemed annoyed about needing to attend have come to understand that we are trying to help their children become more responsible for their actions.

It is essential for parents to understand that school staff members want students to make choices that result in positive outcomes—exactly what parents want. In my role as counselor, I try to enhance cooperation among parents, staff, and students. In a nonjudgmental manner, I inquire about conflicts that students might be struggling with at home and are reflected in what they are doing at school. To best assist a student, we must get a total picture of the dynamics at home.

Using the team approach, the parents, students, teachers, RTP administrator, and principal have all helped tremendously in my effectiveness as a counselor. Before RTP was adopted in our school, it seemed to be only the counselor's responsibility to devise interventions needed to help students. Parents frequently chose not to involve themselves in the poor choices of their children at school. Often, they did not see connections between their children's disruptions and family dynamics. Now, with their participation in intervention team meetings, *all* of the people most important in influencing a child work together. This dynamic combination significantly impacts the child. The counselor is a part of the team. No longer is it the responsibility of the counselor alone to deal with children who make poor choices at school.

During intervention team meetings, parents see the caring attitude of school staff. It has made my job as counselor much easier to solicit the support of parents for the efforts of school staff. Defensive and angry parents have become much more receptive and open to follow-up on RTP referrals in the home. The partnership between home and school is a wonderful bond helping children become more successful and secure. At this point, I certainly appreciate the benefits of the Responsible Thinking Process at Casa Blanca Community School. My main role now is following up on successful interventions, rather than constantly dealing with daily crises.

Why We Are Not There Yet

Scott Bogner
Principal
Evart High School
Evart, Michigan

The Responsible Thinking Process has made an immediate difference in the climate of our school, even though we have not been using the process as well as it could be used. We have implemented the process, hired an RTC coordinator, and received support from all parties concerned, yet we are still not "there." The difference in our school since we began the process is testimony that even if you are not there yet, the process works.

There have been several indications that not everyone is using RTP at our school. Recently I heard comments and concerns from students and staff members that helped me realize we needed more work to better understand both the theory and the process. So I asked Ed to help us pinpoint solutions to our problems. I am writing this chapter to help staff at some schools recognize that they are not there yet, and to help staff at other schools recognize that they have become masters at using the process. As educators, we owe it to our students to use the process as it was designed.

I like to ask students what they think about RTP. At first, their answers consisted of statements about how stupid it is and how it won't work anyway. After a few weeks of seeing RTP in action, the students' comments changed focus. There was one concern that came through loud and clear: the perception that some staff members were not using the process. The students wanted the process to be used consistently. It had not taken long for the students to know what was *supposed* to be done by staff. When the RTP questions were not asked, students felt that they did not *choose* to go to the RTC, but, rather, were *sent*. Having the perception that they were sent seemed to have adverse effects on the negotiation process. Students were naturally defensive, because they felt that they were not given a chance to make effective choices. Consequently, students looked at the process as a way of being controlled. Most of the students felt that if RTP were used correctly, it would be fair. They did not see the RTC as a place where they were punished, but as a place where they could get help. From such comments, I knew that we had succeeded in establishing RTP as a way to help students deal with problems. Making sure that all staff members were using the process was our biggest challenge to RTP's success.

Students have accepted the use of RTP in stride and have adjusted quite well. Staff members have had more difficulty understanding the process. They are committed to helping students, and most would agree that RTP and PCT are sound and good for students. But it is difficult for people to change the way they have done things and to digest new theories at the same time. Our staff recognized that we needed to change the way we dealt with students and discipline, and they were involved in the decision to adopt RTP. The implementation of RTP requires individuals to evaluate the way they run their classrooms and how they deal with student disruptions. As educators, we have been taught that people can be controlled, and that if we yell loudly enough, students will respond. PCT teaches instead that each person is an individual control system designed to think for himself or herself. For some staff, it is difficult to not yell and tell. They have a desire to control others even after they find it increasingly difficult to apply the traditional disciplinary techniques that educators have used. Adopting a system where students are allowed to make choices and not feeling responsible for students' choices are difficult for some staff.

Changing the way people think and helping them to internalize new ideas are always major challenges. I have witnessed teachers trying to control students instead of allowing the students to make choices. Some teachers have been using the process and asking the RTP questions some of the time but yelling and telling the rest of the time. Questions came up daily about the application of RTP in particular situations; our staff meetings became dominated by discussions of concerns about RTP. Each issue, when analyzed, dealt with control. Some staff members still believed that there should be consequences imposed for certain violations of the rules. So we constantly had to return to the basic ideas of RTP and PCT. Even though staff members could recognize the change in climate, they still had a difficult time pinpointing the reasons.

We reviewed various situations that arose and tried to see how they would fit with RTP. At times, some staff thought that the old method of controlling students offered a better option for dealing with problems. It seemed very easy to go back to punishing students and expecting them to change. I found myself asking the staff the RTP questions, because I seemed to be doing all of the thinking. I want staff members to think the same way that we want to help our students think. Besides discussing RTP at staff meetings, we have role-played situations that have occurred in classrooms throughout our school. This role-playing has helped clarify procedures and also has helped me recognize the need for continuing work.

I believe that it is important for the building administrator to be out and about in the school, listening and observing. I was always one to be around the action, so this activity was not new to me. While I am in the hallways, I can easily overhear whether the process is being used. Also, I try to get into the RTC every day to work with students there. While I work with them to resolve their current problems, I ask them about the process. I listen to what they have to say and use their comments to try to get better at using RTP. Being out and about enables me to get a pretty good idea of how things are going.

As we continued to progress in the use of the process, we found it necessary to hold intervention meetings. We had many questions about intervention meetings. The question

that seemed to constantly surface was "What are we supposed to do at this meeting?" How could we help a student
be successful if we were unsure of the proper way to run an
intervention meeting? We felt that the intervention meeting
is an important part of the RTP process, and we wanted to
make sure that we did it correctly.

The most exciting part of this process has been the
progress we have seen with some of our "frequent flyers."
We have our share of students who use the RTC frequently.
There have been very positive results with many of the students who have had difficulty adjusting to the process.
These are mainly students who have experienced the traditional methods of discipline and have never had to think
for themselves or be responsible when dealing with their
problems. They simply took their punishment and waited
out the adults. Now we have those kids at least thinking
about how to handle situations *before* trouble starts. Some
students have gone from being frequent flyers to rarely visiting the RTC. They have improved academically and, more
importantly, have made some connections with adults who
help them through some of the rough moments. Our frequent flyers generally see the RTC as a place where they get
help and are respected. It is powerful to witness a student
transform from a person in constant conflict to a person
who deals more responsibly with his or her problems.

As we continue to learn more about the process, we learn
that there is much more to learn. It has become clear to me
that there is a need to understand PCT at a deeper level.
Our teachers and support staff are working hard at implementing the process, and they are seeing results. In order
to reach the next level, which is to become proficient at
using the process and to do so with a clear understanding
of the underlying theory, we need more knowledge. We
need to strengthen our commitment to doing this thing
correctly. We need more practice applying the concepts as
Ed presents them. We need to refocus on what is good for
our students. We have made the decision to recommit to
RTP. At a high school where the attitude has generally been

to do things to students, we have made significant progress toward changing the way we do business. Our goal is to be certified in the Responsible Thinking Process, because it is the right way to treat students. We want to be a school where students are treated with respect and are taught to think for themselves.

The Untrained Beagle

Al Kullman
Principal
Evart Middle School
Evart, Michigan

One of my favorite sayings as a football coach is that "insanity is doing the same thing over and over but expecting different results." Using yell-and-tell discipline is insane. I knew this before I was hired as the Evart Middle School principal. I had first learned this important lesson when I started teaching, and it was later reinforced when my classroom was directly across from the principal's office. I was familiar with Ed Ford's program and developed a strong expectation of mutual respect in my classroom. I quickly discovered that the stronger the relationship I had with students, the easier it was to solve problems. Children can see straight through adults who do not want to develop relationships with them.

As a new teacher at Evart Junior High/High School, I enthusiastically presented RTP at a staff meeting. They liked it. I was hired the next fall by Evart Public Schools to be the new middle school principal. At that time, Evart schools were going through some significant changes. A new high school (grades 9–12) was built. The junior high/high school was transformed into the present middle school (grades 5–8). There were also many personnel changes, including new staff, teaching assignments, and classrooms. For many, it was a time of excitement; for some, it was a time of concern.

It was at this same time that many in the district (teachers, parents, staff) were unhappy with the present discipline approach. The perception of many was that discipline procedures were inconsistent. In fact, a district-wide discipline committee was formed to recommend changes. As the new middle school principal, I saw this as the perfect opportunity to implement RTP as a model for the district.

The entire middle school staff agreed to implement RTP on the first day of school. The results were almost instantaneous. Teachers noticed greater support from the administration than in the past. Students noticed that all adults were following a consistent discipline program that focused on mutual respect. The climate of the middle school was dramatically different; it was much calmer and more focused. The changes were so noticeable that the discipline committee recommended a district-wide implementation of RTP. Presently, RTP is a K–12 program that has been implemented on the buses as well.

Year two of RTP in the middle school started out as expected, positive and working smoothly. We continued to talk about RTP in staff meetings, shared stories of our successes, and continued to review the process. Our shared vision was that RTP would get easier and become second nature for all of us. We predicted fewer RTC referrals and had far greater expectations than the year before. However, as the year progressed, RTC referrals continued to be higher than predicted. We were frustrated and unsure of what to do next. We began to question whether we were really using RTP correctly, and whether the RTC was structured appropriately. We had reached a plateau and could not figure out where to go next. We began to look closely at each component of RTP and the RTC. I questioned staff and students and concluded that:

- we had drifted from the questioning process
- there was too much nonsense in the RTC

- we were accepting cookie-cutter plans
- we didn't understand intervention

We were clueless and frustrated about what to do next. I took a deep breath and talked with Ed Ford. He and Tom Bourbon arrived at Evart Middle School about three weeks later. They came to evaluate where we were with RTP and to address our concerns. Ed and Tom helped us realize that RTP is a process requiring patience, that we would be frustrated at times, that we did need to make adjustments, and that it was OK to ask for help. Most importantly, we learned that this is typical for schools who intend to make RTP a success. Since Ed's visit, we have:

- made a conscious effort to use the questions, since the process is not yet second-nature to us
- moved the RTC to a room that is configured so that the RTC coordinator can see everyone and deal with disruptions
- learned to help students write better, more specific plans
- endeavored to understand the dynamics of intervention teams

I raise hunting beagles. It's not uncommon for a young beagle to start running rabbits at a young age, sometimes three or four months. By age one or two, a good beagle can often look like a field champion. But on some days, that beagle will look as if he has never seen or smelled a rabbit. By age three, a good hunting beagle begins to mature. He becomes more consistent, looking like a polished hunter, and he rarely loses a rabbit's track. However, there are still days when the beagle looks suspect. Nonetheless, a good hunter is always patient with his young dog, never gives up, and sticks with what he knows to work. The good hunter always draws from his previous successful experiences.

I think we are like a one-year-old beagle at Evart Middle School. On some days, the RTP process looks like a champion; on others, it's questionable. Evart Middle School will continue to improve our use of the Responsible Thinking Process. We will be patient and persistent, and we will learn from our experiences. Presently, we are an untrained beagle, striving to become a polished field champion.

Our First Year Using RTP

Kathy Welsh
Assistant Principal
Desert Mirage Elementary School
Pendergast Elementary School District
Glendale, Arizona

Before we adopted RTP, I think we were like most other schools. Things were going reasonably well, with good instruction taking place, but there were concerns and questions about the consistency and effectiveness of discipline, and the amount of time being spent on it. We wanted to be able to focus more on teaching. Our parent group supported the idea of looking into a discipline process because they felt that detention was not changing student behavior. I called Ed Ford and asked him to talk to our faculty about the Responsible Thinking Process. After his presentation, our staff agreed that we should implement RTP. We shared information with the school board and answered their questions; the board and superintendent approved our putting RTP in place. We were very fortunate that the board, superintendent, parents, and teachers were so supportive; we encountered no roadblocks.

Before school started, our principal, Becky Osuna, and I met with Rich Wellbrock. Rich was chosen to be the responsible thinking classroom teacher. The three of us met several times to discuss the process, the RTP questions, and how students would need to work through their plans. Some discussions focused on Rich's attitude when working with the students, helping them to take responsibility and to think through their problems. We also discussed how we could support the program, support each other, and make sure that Rich would have administrative support.

During orientation week, the staff spent one morning talking about the specific ways students deal with others. We distinguished between those that interfere with student learning and those that annoy teachers; we made a list of those that interfere with learning. Copies of *Discipline for Home and School, Book One* and *Book Two* were given to each teacher to read. Then Ed spent a day with the faculty explaining the philosophy and the process. We sent a letter home to give parents an overview of RTP. We held four parent workshops, organized by grade level; thus, parents were able to learn about RTP and ask questions. Ed came to one parent workshop and worked with us to clarify some ideas.

After Ed met with the faculty, we started using the RTP questions, the RTC, and the student plan making process. In the beginning, some plans were well-written, some students wrote what they thought the teacher wanted to hear, and some didn't write actual plans at all. As the students wrote plans, we learned more about writing appropriate plans, and we began to learn how to question the students to help them write meaningful plans. Right from the beginning, Becky, Rich, our counselor, Kathy Johnson, and I have spent time talking about how to deal with issues by keeping the solutions within the parameters of the Responsible Thinking Process. This dialogue was and still is important, because it keeps us focused on the process. Throughout the year, we have used faculty meetings to talk through the process, hear each other's questions, and learn where our strengths are, as well as which areas need more clarification or support from the administration. Such dialoguing is key to keeping the process strong.

As we have worked through the process this year, we have learned several things. It is beneficial to have a certified teacher and an aide in the responsible thinking classroom. In fact, we would not have received the support we did without a certified teacher. The parents, teachers, and students responded better in the beginning, knowing that there was a teacher in the room. However, Angela Cantu, our aide, has become an integral part of the success of the program and is highly respected for the work she is doing in the RTC. Rich and Angela work as a team, which is important for the students and teachers to know, giving credibility to all plans written in the RTC. Having two people who work together this well makes the process and the room run more smoothly.

From the beginning of the year, the intervention team (Becky, Kathy, Rich, the classroom teacher, and I) have been meeting with parents of students who disrupt frequently. As we discussed working with different students and how to support the students and their classroom teachers, we began to understand that there were many situations in which the intervention team needed to be involved. There were still students who were consistently disruptive. These students were wanting something, and we realized the need to talk it through as a team with their parents. The results of intervention team meetings have been very positive, and the parents have been very supportive. Kathy Johnson is working with several students, and Rich Wellbrock is seeing some students throughout the day based on plans developed during these meetings. Involved parents have been given copies of *Book One* and are supporting the program at home. We are learning to use the intervention team more effectively and are realizing that it is a very powerful tool.

It has become apparent how important negotiating is to the process. This is something we did not spend enough time on at the beginning of the year. Teachers need to take it seriously and to realize how powerful it can be within the process. As we continued to work through plans with students, we began to realize what happens during negotiating, and how much teachers can learn about students. Here is where teachers learn what students are thinking and help students understand their (teachers') expectations. Here, teachers build rapport with students and guide the students in thinking about what is acceptable behavior in the classroom and what choices they can make so they are successful. We began to understand negotiating better as we began to understand plans better.

We also began to understand that we would have to give some of the students time. Many students understood the process immediately, and some students had to write a plan only once. However, as we worked with more difficult students, we talked about these students having been in trouble with the same problems for a long time, so it might take time to change. We learned that we had to take many baby steps with these students, but as we worked with them, we did see positive changes. We saw students start talking positively about themselves, and we saw a decrease in the length and frequency of their tantrums. This took time, and while we now know that the process is working, there is still frustration when a student or parent is not cooperating. Given this frustration, some teachers have considered going back to other ways of dealing with problems, or developing systems outside the Responsible Thinking Process, or becoming punitive. Talking things through helps everyone stay focused and thinking about how to use RTP in a variety of situations. We do not want to get into power struggles with students; rather, we want to work within the process and help students accept responsibility. We are working to give the students respect and let go of controlling.

Throughout the year, we have made changes that benefit students and teachers. We have changed the forms that teachers use to send students to the RTC, and we have changed the questions on the sheets that the students fill out so they are more age-appropriate. During Ed's visit, he made suggestions that helped us refine the process. He suggested setting up areas in the cafeteria and on the playground for students who are returning after writing plans. Students have the opportunity to follow their plans, then move back into the everyday life of the cafeteria and playground.

We are seeing wonderful changes on the campus. The office is quiet and calm—in fact, the whole campus is calmer. Students are treating teachers with more respect. We have seen marked improvements by some very difficult students. The teachers say that they have more time to teach. We are pleased with the progress we are making, and we are looking forward to next year.

Getting Started and Staying on Track

Dave Anderson
Principal
Sahuaro Elementary School
Washington Elementary School District
Phoenix, Arizona

When I announced to my faculty that discipline had surfaced as our primary improvement goal, I observed mixed reactions. "Are you sure?" was the look I saw on many faces. The improvement process in our school district is rather elaborate, and quite scientific, and I must say that I, too, was a little surprised. At this point, however, we were in too deep not to trust the results of the process.

So we embarked on the research phase. A research team of staff and parents was formed. Their job was to clarify exactly what was not working at Sahuaro School in terms of student discipline, analyze our current discipline practices, and examine the literature to identify critical attributes for effective school discipline. The research team also made visits to a number of schools to observe various programs in action. Two qualities were identified early on as being uniquely important for the success of a discipline process at Sahuaro School. It was clear that the staff desired school-wide consistency with an appropriate level of teacher flexibility. Teachers were frustrated by their lack of success using punishments and rewards to change student behavior; they were searching for a process that focused on intrinsic self-discipline. These two qualities and 13 critical attributes of effective discipline practices identified from the literature were merged to form a discipline process profile—sort of a shopping list. Now that we knew what we were looking for, it was time to find it.

The research team broke into smaller groups to begin searching. The hunt included school visitations, phone conferences with personnel from distant schools, and an examination of articles written about specific plans being implemented throughout the country.

I remember one particular research team meeting very clearly. As we were sharing information obtained in our search, one group reported that they were extremely impressed with a certain school they had just visited. "There was such an atmosphere of respect", they said. "We've never experienced anything like it, and their discipline plan fits our profile like a glove." As they continued to share, a member from one of the other groups stopped them in mid-sentence: "Wait a minute. What is the name of the discipline plan you are talking about?" "The Responsible Thinking Process." "You're not going to believe this. but we visited a school using that same plan, and we, too, were struck by the high level of respect between students and teachers." So RTP gained the attention of the entire research team. A few months later, after making several presentations to the faculty and community, the Sahuaro site council unanimously approved adopting the Responsible Thinking Process.

We had most of the fall to work out the details before officially starting RTP in January. Ed Ford was brought in for an all-day training of the staff and parents. The research team became the discipline core team and picked up a few additional members. Their goals were to become "experts" themselves, to plan and carry out training for the staff and students, and to work out the specifics of Sahuaro School's plan. One of the core team's first jobs was to develop a brochure explaining the process. This proved advantageous because it forced the team to define the major aspects, solidifying what they were learning. The brochure became a handy tool that was used (and still is being used) to explain the process to parents. Staff training was ongoing throughout the fall. Each staff member received a copy of *Discipline for Home and School, Book One*. Teachers were encouraged to practice the RTP questioning process, even though the responsible thinking classroom was not yet set up. The students also learned the process gradually in this way. Faculty and parents were asked for input periodically as the core team roughed out the various components. When December arrived, we were ready to do the formal training with students. Grades K–6 toured the RTC and were given opportunities to ask questions. Originally, when we slated January 4 as our official implementation date, there was concern that students would find the mid-year transition difficult. In reality, the gradual learning process that occurred from September to December actually made the adjustment easier for students and teachers.

January 4 brought with it a certain degree of anticipation. Was RTP going to work? The first student showed up in the RTC at about 10:00 a.m. that first morning. By the end of the first week, 40 to 50 students, out of a total enrollment of 620, were visiting daily. Renita Steinmann and Annette Munster, our RTC teachers, were doing a fine job, and the majority of our staff appeared to be comfortable with the process. As the initial weeks passed, it was obvious that our training efforts had paid off.

As we approached the two-month mark, we had reached a plateau. The "frequent flyers" had identified themselves, and much of the talk around campus focused on them. Teachers began expressing their concern that students were returning from the RTC with plans identical to ones they had written previously—that students were writing rote responses. The core team was meeting regularly to address questions and concerns. A moderate percentage of the staff had begun to develop some feelings of frustration: "this process isn't working" was the cry. At this point, some of the faculty began to slip back into the punishment/telling mode: "If the students won't follow the rules on their own, I'll force them to comply." The core team struggled with the question, "How can we get the students to think on a deeper level and to demonstrate genuine commitment to the plans they write?" I noticed one more thing. The RTC was becoming the Responsible Thinking Process in and of itself. We were losing sight of the broader, more powerful applications of RTP and perceptual control theory. "The RTC isn't fixing the students," some said.

At this point, we needed a jump-start to propel us beyond the level where we found ourselves stuck. Ed Ford and Tom Bourbon agreed to spend a day on our campus to evaluate our progress. They spent time observing the RTC, classrooms, and common areas. Students and staff were questioned in an attempt to determine their depth of understanding. At the end of the day, Ed and Tom met with the faculty. This proved to be a valuable experience for two reasons. First, we were able to identify specific problem areas: negotiations and lingering directive behaviors by staff. We discovered that we were missing relationship-building opportunities during the negotiation process. We were also accepting plans that had little or no substance. Students often restated the rules as their responses, rather than thinking about concrete solutions. Staff members were not expecting them to think and were not offering alternatives or suggestions to help strengthen their plans. In addition, we were still directing/telling students what to do, especially in the common areas on campus. The evaluation by Ed and Tom benefited us in a second way. As they talked with the faculty, they expressed their amazement at how far we had come in just two short months. Tom stated that every student he talked to could have written a book on the Responsible Thinking Process. This was a big boost to our staff, who had been working very hard to make the process work. It gave us a perspective we desperately needed—like hiking 10 miles to the top of a high peak, then looking back over the landscape at our accomplishment. We *had* made progress—a *lot* of progress.

I suppose that the plateau we experienced is the point at which some schools begin a downward spiral to failure. It is very easy to fall back into the trap of punishments and rewards (cause-effect). The educational pendulum of new ideas swings back and forth, and with each pass, it carries hope that disappears later, as trust begins to wane and apathy sets in. We start to ask, "Is it possible to really change anything?"

I believe several key factors have kept us focused on making the Responsible Thinking Process work. Most critical is a genuine belief in the foundation on which RTP is built: perceptual control theory. How can one argue that teaching children to think is not a good thing? I recently had a conference with two parents who work in the state corrections industry. They said that when they ask inmates why they chose to break the law and go to jail, the reply is almost always, "I didn't choose to come here." Did they not know beforehand that breaking the law often leads to incarceration? Most of my first graders can make that connection. Knowing that you're building a program based on a solid foundation helps you weather the storm that will surely come. The second key factor is persistence, unfortunately almost a lost concept in this world of one-hour time slots. It's important to realize that implementing RTP is a continuing process. There is no such thing as a process that runs itself. A good process requires maintenance. The last important catalyst in getting RTP off the ground has been the discipline core team. This amazing group of staff and parents has been invaluable. As they discuss RTP issues and solve problems during core team meetings, I sit there and marvel at the discussions going on, at the thinking that is taking place, at the constant screening of solutions through the PCT sieve, and at the members' sincerity and dedication to making RTP work at our school. It's because of them that we are on the peak looking back.

Although RTP is an ongoing process, in one respect it produced almost instant results. Sahuaro School had been averaging 30 tardies per day, a constant thorn in our side. As the core team discussed the problem, we realized that at the elementary level, the parents were responsible for 80% of "untimely arrivals" (as we euphemistically called them). But how could we hold students responsible for the actions of their parents? We developed a Tardy Plan for Parents (shown on page 112). When a student is late to school a given number of times, I call the parents to determine the cause. If the student is responsible for the tardy, say by refusing to get out of bed or by taking a "scenic route" to school, he or she reports to the RTC the next time he or she is tardy to write a plan. But if the parents are responsible for the tardy, I schedule a conference with them. I ask them a few questions in a non-threatening way and write down their responses on their plan. Parents sign it when we are finished. By addressing the responsible parties directly, whether they are children or adults, we've been able to reduce the number of tardies to about four per day. That thorn is much less painful.

TARDY PLAN FOR PARENTS

Student's name _____

Date _____

1. What happens when your child walks into class late?

2. What is happening at home in the morning that is preventing your child from getting to school on time?

3. What are your goals for your child's academic success?

4. How do your child's tardies affect the goals?

5. How will you change your morning routine to prevent future tardies?

Parent's signature _____

Date _____

You Have RTP Implemented . . . How Do You Keep It Going?

Don Nelson
Principal
Page Middle School
Page, Arizona

Vicki Wright
RTC Teacher
Page Middle School
Page, Arizona

A school that has implemented the Responsible Thinking Process has taken a giant step toward creating a safe and orderly climate for learning. The students in such a school are functioning in a system that helps them learn to make better personal and social decisions on a daily basis, resulting in a better learning environment.

Our intent here is to offer some practical ideas on how to keep the process going after it has been implemented. One thing is certain: after being involved with RTP for a few years, we have discovered that every day is an ongoing learning process.

In our experience, RTP is received better than other discipline processes because it is perceived as "fair." Expectations are known up front, students have more than one chance to learn, and parents can understand and contribute to the process in the home. Continuing contact with the parents is vital to keeping the process alive and well. This contact is best maintained by providing training sessions for parents throughout the school year. Newsletters and bulletins sent home with students can be used to communicate with the parents concerning the process. And when the process calls for conferences with parents, additional communication takes place. Word of mouth from highly trained and enthusiastic staff members also helps communication with the community at large.

Students need to be apprised of expectations, rules, boundaries, and consequences of their choices on a daily basis. Each new student needs to be informed about how the process works and should be taken to visit the responsible thinking classroom. An introduction to the process and a visit to the RTC should always be included when elementary students attend middle school orientation. One of the remarkable things about RTP is the fact that the students learn how the process works faster than anyone else!

Staff training is ongoing. It is very important to remember that "anything that is not monitored becomes optional." The only option involved in using RTP is each staff member's decision as to the point at which he or she will choose to begin the process. Once the questioning starts, the process can't be short-circuited, compromised, watered down, or changed on the personal whim of any staff member. To insure consistency in the process, formal training prior to the school year, *every* year, is a must. New teachers' training is more involved than veteran staff training. Also, it is crucial that RTP be addressed regularly in faculty meetings, so it becomes the accepted way of doing business on campus.

Staff dialogue needs to be encouraged as the environment on campus changes. Defined procedures are a must to maintain consistency, but realizing that nothing except change itself remains constant, staff members must engage in open discussion as necessary to decide how to deal with new challenges. Again, consistency is the key. Classroom teachers, bus drivers, cafeteria workers, and other staff members have specific rules and procedures to be followed in their respective areas, but consistency on general issues like running, chewing gum, tardies, hands on/off policy, etc. are dealt with more successfully when all staff members are consistent in their treatment of the common issues.

If the RTC is full, that doesn't mean that the process isn't working. If the RTC is empty, that doesn't mean that the process isn't working. However, there are three people who can tell you when the process isn't working: the RTC teacher, the RTC aide, and (especially) a student involved in the process: "I didn't get a warning." "He just said to go to the RTC." "I don't know why I'm here." "I just walked in the class and she said, 'Go to the RTC.'" "Mr. Graves didn't ask me the RTP questions." These are indications that a staff member isn't using the process. Either the administrator or the RTC teacher needs to visit with the staff member whose use of the process is questionable. Sometimes both the RTC teacher and the administrator can conference with the individual staff member. Most of the time, failure to follow the process is due to oversight, lack of communication, or taking a short cut. Simply reviewing the reasons for following the process and the reasons that it has been so successful usually will solve the problem. In worst-case scenarios, a teacher who is having difficulty might be asked to observe a teacher who uses the process effectively.

The most difficult staff member to work with is probably one who wants to "do something to the student." "He should be punished." "She made a bad choice and something has to happen to her." In such a situation, the staff member should be dealt with in the same way that students are dealt with: ask questions respectfully, try to determine what the individual might be controlling for, and work to help the staff member make a plan to solve his or her problem. Nothing succeeds like success, and once the individual finds that RTP works better than any other process, he or she will usually come around. Of course, old habits die hard sometimes.

What about students who choose the RTC so often that they are referred to as "frequent flyers"? There aren't many, but each school has a few who might require extraordinary intervention due to personal problems which exceed the norm. RTP actually helps to identify students needing special attention, and the RTC staff can coordinate interventions to address these at-risk students' needs. If such cases are handled properly, the Responsible Thinking Process will not be compromised.

In order to keep RTP (or any other process) going, it is important to celebrate success. And there *will* be success! As long as teachers are teaching and students are learning, success is present. Keep students, parents, and staff informed as to statistics in the area of discipline. This helps to perpetuate and create support for the process. It is important always to focus on, and to communicate to everyone, that fewer disruptions, less disrespect, and less disobedience equal more learning. That means students learning more, and more students learning. That is why we are in this business.

It is also important to remember that the Responsible Thinking Process is about helping students make good choices on a daily basis at school. RTP is not only about students and staff, it is institutional. When the process becomes "institutionalized" ("That's the way we've always done it."), then the school climate is affected in a very positive way. The process should not be taken for granted. To keep the process going requires constant vigilance: observe, listen, discuss, always looking for a way to improve, a way to be more effective. A safe and orderly climate is a mandatory prerequisite to learning and being successful in America's classrooms. Our students' future depends on it, and our nation's future depends on our students.

What It Takes to Get and Keep RTP Going

Above all else, the right people:
• Administrators sold on the program
• RTC staff who must be patient, organized, calm, and dependable
• Staff at all levels willing to follow through with established RTP procedures
• Someone willing to work with staff who need assistance with classroom management

Communication:
- Comprehensive staff training
- Student education about the process
- Well-defined procedures
- Guidelines on which types of disruptions are to be considered RTC issues

And an adequately equipped RTC:
- Study carrels
- Two desks with chairs for staff
- Computer to record referrals
- Telephone with outside line
- Student file folders and cabinets to store them
- Log book
- Forms (referrals, plans, parent notifications, student monitor sheets, etc.)
- Student demographics records
- Student schedules
- Staff master schedule
- Copies of RTC rules and "Life Skills" mounted in each carrel
- School calendar
- Desk clock (there should not be a clock on the wall)
- *Lots* of pencils
- Miscellaneous classroom supplies, including pens, colored pencils, dictionary/thesaurus, calculator, paper, reading material, stapler, ruler, glue, protractor, correction fluid, highlighters, note pads, scissors, and trash can

Chapter 16
Developing Personal Responsibility in the Disabled Child

Erin Powell
Special Education Teacher
Gateway Elementary School
Creighton Elementary School District
Phoenix, Arizona

A real test of the validity of the Responsible Thinking Process for many educators is how well the process works with special ed students. As I've traveled throughout the U.S. and overseas, I've heard both teachers and administrators claim over and over again that many special ed children cannot think and decide for themselves how to deal responsibly with their peers and adults. Some educators claim that a number of these children really can't distinguish right from wrong, and so teachers and parents are held responsible for the children's actions.

Erin Powell, without a doubt one of the most competent special ed teachers I've ever met, at one time believed that her students were limited with regard to personal responsibility. For many years, she trained others in the use of behavioral modification. But Erin was willing to challenge her own beliefs and what she had learned from others. I often recall the day I was visiting Erin's class when little Jimmy refused to line up. I was overwhelmed by what she did with Jimmy and the other children. Even to write these words brings tears to my eyes.

Erin had seven students in class that day, all between five and eight years old. Jane was six years old, with mild mental retardation. She tried to speak in complete sen-

tences, but others had great difficulty understanding what she said. Vanessa and Amy were seven years old and were also mildly mentally retarded. Sheryl was an eight-year-old non-verbal autistic child who used communication overlays and signing to communicate. Oscar was also an autistic eight-year-old. He communicated verbally using at least three-word sentences. Eddy was five years old, with severe mental retardation. He was microcephalic and used a wheelchair that gave him maximum support. He could roll on the floor to go small distances in the classroom, and other individuals pushed him in his wheelchair. He was working to express himself by using a switch connected to a loop tape. Finally, there was six-year-old Jimmy, who was labeled severely mentally retarded. He had difficulty speaking but was beginning to use single-word phrases. Jimmy used a walker to move around.

Erin asked the students to line up for lunch. All except Jimmy formed a line; Jimmy started walking around the room. Erin guided him to a wall with a poster depicting the classroom rules and a board with "Yes" and "No" communication symbols on it. Using RTP, she guided him through the questions, and Jimmy finally committed to following the rules and began to make his plan, using the symbols to communicate. While Jimmy was working with Erin, the other students waited patiently in line listening to Jimmy. There wasn't one disruption. When Jimmy was done answering Erin's questions, excited by having made a plan, he turned to walk toward the other students in line. In his excitement, he bumped into a desk, laughed, then took his place at the end of the line. He was smiling at us and, unintentionally, bumped into the person in front of him. Erin suggested to Jimmy that he take his place at the front of the line and lead the class to the cafeteria.

Jimmy was so proud that he was being responsible by leading the class to the cafeteria, he often looked back and smiled at the adults. Sometimes when he looked back, he bumped into a post or a wall. And when he did, he would laugh and then proceed onward. Meanwhile, the rest of the class followed Jimmy, staying in line without any adult telling them what to do. Jane, hardly reaching the top of Eddy's wheelchair, was pushing him while staying in line. This was her classroom job. At the cafeteria, some of the children, on their own or with some assistance, took their appropriate seats at the table. Others went through the line to get food for those who couldn't manage it on their own. Remarkable!

So many educators suppose that children like those in Erin's classroom could not do many of the things they did on that day (or any other day). They couldn't learn to respect the rights of other students. They couldn't learn to help others when the need presented itself. I saw, firsthand, how children with severe disabilities could be successful and responsible for their actions using higher-order thinking. On that day, Erin Powell taught me far more than I could have ever taught her.—Ed Ford

I have always taught self-contained Varying Exceptionalities classrooms. I've worked with primary, intermediate, and middle school aged students, who function mostly in the mild to severe mental retardation range. Among these students are children with physical impairments, visual impairments, autism, and medical fragility. All of my students are mainstreamed into the general curriculum at some level; some go daily to the regular education classrooms, while others go a few times a week. All are included in music, art, physical education, special events, and other non-academic programs. Having my students included in the school community is a major goal; therefore, it is important that my students participate in RTP at our school.

I heard Ed Ford speak about RTP three years ago. I became excited about the possibilities of RTP because I was tired of token economy, group and individual contingency, and response-cost programs that I had learned about in my college behavioral modification courses. It took *so* much time and resources to develop and implement them, and once I got them started, including the training of staff and students, and they seemed to be working well, they would always lose their effectiveness. Before my introduction to RTP, I thought that using behavioral modification techniques was the only way to manage my class. As I learned about RTP, I kept thinking to myself, "How are *my* students going to be included in this?" At the time, half of my students did not know how to comprehend questions, much less answer them appropriately, and some of my students were completely nonverbal. I asked Ed Ford for advice on how I could implement this program in my classroom. Ed replied,"The same way as with other students." And he told me that I should have high expectations for my students. I took his advice and developed ways to adapt the program so that my students could participate.

In order to implement RTP with my students who did not comprehend how to answer questions, I adapted the RTP questioning process by simplifying the questions, supplying visual aids, and adding role-playing situations. Here is an example showing how I adapted the process for one of my students. Jimmy was a six-year-old boy who was severely mentally retarded and physically impaired. He used a walker to ambulate. He talked using one-word utterances to express his needs, and he had difficulty answering basic questions related to daily events. Jimmy sometimes would disobey directions and hit other people, bringing attention to himself. One day, the students in my class were asked to line up to go to lunch, and Jimmy started walking in circles and hitting the students in line while laughing.

Teacher: What are you doing?

Jimmy: (Looks at teacher while laughing.)

Teacher: Are you hitting other students? (She pretends to hit herself.)

Jimmy: (Points to "Yes" on communication overlay.)

Teacher: What are the rules? (Points to our classroom rules chart with realistic pictures paired with written rules.)

Jimmy: (Points to appropriate picture-rule pairing on chart.)

Teacher: That's right, Jimmy. We keep our hands to our-selves. (Teacher pats her hands on her lap to illustrate rule.)

Teacher: What happens when you break the rules? Do you hurt other people? (Mimicking the faces of the students who were hit.)

Jimmy: (Points to "No" on communication overlay.)

Teacher: Yes, it *does* hurt. Can you tell me, 'Yes'?

Jimmy: (Points to "Yes" on communication overlay.)

Teacher: Is this what you want? Do you want to hurt your friends?

Jimmy: (Points to "No" on communication overlay.)

Teacher: What are you going to do now? Are you going to line up with your hands to yourself? (Pretending to line up this way.)

Jimmy: (Points to "Yes" on communication overlay.)

Teacher: What happens if you disrupt again? Do you go to the responsible thinking classroom?

Jimmy: (Points to "Yes" on communication overlay, then gets in line and stands still while waiting to leave.)

Jimmy needed visual aids, help from me, and role-play-ing to handle the RTP questioning. This assistance enabled him to comprehend the questions. He was the one who was controlling his experiences, who was thinking about what he wanted. His actions were merely what he used to achieve his goals; his actions were *not* his goals. I was no longer forcing him to change his behavior by trying to control him through reinforcements. Instead, by using the RTP ques-tioning process, I was teaching him to think about how he could achieve his goals without hurting others. As time went on, Jimmy became able to understand and answer the questions verbally using two-word utterances.

For my nonverbal students, I have created various over-lays for their communication devices that facilitate their answering the RTP questions. The number of locations on each student's overlay depend on his or her comprehen-sion ability. Sean, a five-year-old labeled severely mentally retarded, used a two-grid overlay with "Yes" and "No" pro-grammed on his communication device. Cindy, an 11-year-old multiply-handicapped child, used a nine-grid overlay on her communication device. She had locations programmed with the following rules: "Keep hands to yourself," "Be nice to our friends," and "Follow directions." She also had on her overlay: "Yes," "No," "RTC," "I am ready to work," "I like this plan," and "I need a break." Sharon, an eight-year-old autistic child, used a 32-grid overlay to communicate. Phrases on Sharon's overlay referred to her most common disruptions (such as running and not following directions), "Yes," "No," the classroom rules, and alternative behaviors that she could choose instead of disrupting.

Even though it took some time to teach the students how to comprehend the questions, I found that it was time well spent. They—including students with severe disabilities—were learning to think for themselves while respecting the rights of others. They were becoming responsible for how they treated others while they were trying to achieve what they wanted. At times, it was a matter of asking the initial question: "What are you doing?" Then, I could see the student stop and think about it. For instance, Tammy was a six-year-old with mild mental retardation who spoke using two- to three-word utterances. One day at Story Time, the students were participating in a flannel-board story. Tammy kept jumping up to grab a flannel-board piece, even though it was not her turn. I repeatedly told her to sit down and wait for her turn, but she did not listen. I had slipped back into my old ways of dealing with students. Once I realized this, I waited for the next opportunity. Then, the next time she jumped up to grab a flannel-board piece, I asked her, "What are you doing?" She stopped, dropped the piece, sat down, and said, "Hands to self." Another example: Todd, a multiply-handicapped eight-year-old, was dumping clay onto the floor. I asked him what he was doing, and he stopped dumping the clay onto the floor and resumed playing appropriately. And another example: Sharon, a low-functioning autistic seven-year-old, was running away from the class after being asked to line up. When I asked her what she was doing, she stopped running and joined the line.

Now I am working in a VE classroom with fifth, sixth, and seventh grade aged students. Using RTP has been easier with older students. I still adapt the questions for some students, but they are more mature and able to learn the questioning process quicker. Jennifer, a non-verbal autistic 12-year-old, sometimes hits other people who wear glasses or have hair in their faces. When she hits other people, I go over the RTP questions with her. She uses the classroom rules chart and a nine-grid overlay to express herself. The overlay has phrases like "Yes," "No," "Glasses off," "Move hair," "Move please," "Leave me alone," "I'm mad," and "Can I go away?" Jennifer has learned how to communicate instead of hitting others through the plans she has developed with RTP. Peter is a 12-year-old student with mild mental retardation. Before he came to my class, he had been placed in detention and suspended numerous times from a previous school for skipping classes, stealing, and fighting. His previous school did not use RTP. Within the first month during which he used the process, Peter came to me three times and told me that he was going to fight a person but then remembered his plan. He developed a plan to walk away as soon as he became mad at someone. Peter independently followed his plan using RTP. Because of this, he has avoided at least three fights.

I have been using RTP for three years. Through the years, there have been some frustrations. The hardest thing is getting the staff to use this process *consistently*. As in many self-contained classrooms, the staff turnover rate is high; therefore, I am constantly teaching new people to use RTP. It is hard for people to understand the significance of using the process if they have not gone through training that includes an introduction to perceptual control theory. PCT provides a whole new way to look at individuals and their behaviors, especially for those who have been trained in behavioral modification.

To reduce the time required to teach staff, including instructional aides, speech therapists, occupational therapists, physical therapists, and volunteers, I have found it helpful to provide visual aids and models for staff to use in RTP questioning. I have the questions posted in the room next to the classroom rules chart. The questions are in large lettering. I also give the staff small cards with the questions written on them. These cards go with us when we are out of the room. I walk staff members through the questioning process whenever a disruption occurs. Even though this stops the class activity, it is a learning experience for everyone. Not only does it provide a model for the classroom staff, but it also provides a model for the students.

Another frustration I have encountered is getting parents involved with RTP. It is difficult to teach parents proficiency in using the process. Even though my students' parents sign a discipline policy plan describing how RTP is used in the classroom, and even though I regularly discuss how their children are using the process throughout the year, I have found that most of the parents do not use the process at home. During meetings with parents who have asked for help with their children's home behaviors, I have thought to myself, "What a perfect opportunity to teach RTP." But after I explained RTP and the theory behind it, and left copies of the questions with the parents, I discovered that the parents still were not using the RTP questions at home and, thus, still continued to have disruptions at home. I have come to believe that parents need training in their homes so that they fully understand the process. In such training, the parents should be encouraged to learn the questioning procedures, plan development procedures, and negotiating procedures. After observing the process as used by others, the parents should have opportunities to use the process themselves, initially under the guidance of an expert.

The final frustration I have experienced is that I am currently at a school that does not have a responsible thinking classroom. The RTC is a very important component of RTP, especially for older students. The RTC is a place where the students have an opportunity to work on written plans. It is a place away from the environment where they are disrupting. It is a place that has trained staff to help the students. The RTC is a great place to negotiate students' plans because it is a quiet and safe environment. When I taught at a school with an RTC, the RTC teacher was incredible with my students. She learned how to use communication devices for individual students, she trained her staff on each child's needs, and she knew how to adapt the questions for each student. Because there is no RTC to which my students can choose to go, we have developed a substitute. My students go to a "thinking chair" within the classroom when they disrupt for a second time. This is where they develop and negotiate a verbal plan with staff.

Since we have implemented RTP, I no longer have to spend countless hours developing behavioral modification programs that ultimately lose their effectiveness. I still encounter daily disruptions from students in my classroom. These will always occur. The important difference is that my students are becoming more and more responsible for how they deal with others as they strive to get what they themselves want. I no longer use behavioral modification programs. Controlling and manipulating students is ineffective. I'm teaching my students to think for themselves.

RTP not only allows my students to use their higher-order thought processes—cognitive skills that many people have claimed are not possible for students with severe disabilities—it also allows my students to be responsible for themselves. And is this not the ultimate goal we should strive for with *all* individuals?

Chapter 17
RTP on the Gila River Indian Reservation

Jack Foster
Principal
Casa Blanca Community School
Gila River Indian Reservation
Bapchule, Arizona

During the summer of 1996, I became the principal of Casa Blanca Community School. I knew from being school counselor in previous years that our school needed a more effective discipline program. In previous years, the couch in front of the principal's office was filled before 7:30 a.m. with students to see the principal. After attending a workshop on RTP given by Ed Ford, assessing the school staff, and getting their buy-in, I asked Ed to give us a presentation in August 1996. We immediately began to implement RTP.

When the 1996–97 school year began, our first 30 days were very difficult. Initially, we had 24–30 students choosing to go to the responsible thinking classroom each day. But after a couple of months, the number went down to 15–18 students per day, and during the third and fourth months, it was 12–15. Our progress since then: May 1997, 3–5 RTC students per day; May 1998, 2–3 students per day; December 1998, 0–2 students per day. When our RTC teacher, Ted Huerta, overheard students talking about having an RTC in their play-school at home, he knew that the program was taking hold. After just three months, many of the staff also noticed something different: the students were calmer.

Now, when they come off the buses, the students are smiling and talking happily as they enter the cafeteria. They greet teachers with "Good morning" and smiles. Before RTP, many students were scowling at or even hitting other students. Before the 1996–97 school year, there had been disruptions each day even before school started.

Our food service manager, Emory Caudill, remembers when thrown food, swearing, and noise were standard in the cafeteria. Recently, a student was heard swearing in the lunch line, and Emory had him step behind the counter so he could continue serving. The manager began to ask the RTP questions. After the first question ("What are you doing?"), the student blurted out, "Kicking, and I'm supposed to keep my hands and feet to myself." The cafeteria staff couldn't help but laugh. The student just continued by answering the rest of the questions that he knew were going to be asked. Then he apologized and assured Emory that it wouldn't happen again. He continued to the dining area, acting in an appropriate manner. Before RTP, such disrupters wouldn't talk to staff.

Two monitors eat with the students. Before RTP, we had four monitors and many disruptions. Now, the students choose to follow the rules. They pick up after themselves. When I ask the students in the lunchroom, "Who are the best children in the nation?" all of them raise their hands. The Casa Blanca students feel good about themselves. Three years ago, none of them would have raised a hand. Our special education teacher, Mrs. Krech, has told me that, before RTP, when students were asked, "How are you doing," the reply was either "terrible" or "not good." Recently, when she asked the same question, typical responses were "great," "OK," "fine," and "very good." What a difference from three years ago!

At assemblies, I now put over 300 K–4 students shoulder-to-shoulder in the cafeteria. There are no problems, even in sessions lasting from 45 to 50 minutes. Four years ago, we could have only two classes in an assembly at a time because of the many disruptions. And students come into the library during their lunch and afternoon recesses, read, and monitor themselves and their peers in the "quiet zone." Rarely does the librarian have to ask the RTP questions.

Now, teachers are able to teach full-time. When a student disrupts the first time, the teacher asks the RTP questions; a second disruption means that the student has chosen to go to the RTC. Teachers do not have to yell. Instead, they calmly ask the RTP questions. Once a student has chosen to go to the RTC, the teacher doesn't back down by pleading. The student's choice is final. One student walked into a fourth grade room and said, "Mr. Heywood, you're going to have to write me up. I hit another student. He called me a name." This student knew that he had made a bad choice. This had never happened in the past.

A fourth grade teacher, Mr. Cameron, told me about an incident in which one of his students hit another student. The student was asked, "What are you doing?" He replied, "But he hit me . . ." Again he was asked, "What are you doing?" The student then explained what he did and continued through the process of writing his plan. He wrote, "I should have told the teacher after Mark hit me. If I had to do it over again, I would have told the teacher." This student made a mistake, learned from it, and moved on. This is learning at its finest. RTP does not condemn mistakes. It allows students to learn from them.

Mr. Heywood told me about a student who had been very angry and troublesome for two years. Once, instead of going to tutoring with a smile, he went in frowning, slammed himself into a chair, shouted his first two answers, and said he didn't want to be there. At the time, he was a "frequent flyer" in the RTC but had been making progress. The tutoring teacher, in helping him make a plan to deal with this problem, suggested that if he was going to be disruptive when he came to tutoring, he could just tell her without getting angry and rude. He could choose to go to the RTC to cool off and do his work. He sat up, said he wanted to stay, and got to work. The next time he was called, she could see him thinking about his choices as he got up and gave a faint, sly smile while marching to the tutoring area.

We have a restricted area in the playground for students who have difficulty playing with a large number of students. Very few students disrupt in the regular playground, because they can choose to go to the restricted area. I remember when one student, Jim, came out of the cafeteria and looked out at the main playground, where about 100 students were playing. He looked over at the restricted area and asked if he could have a pass to go to the restricted playground. I could see that he was making a good decision, because he usually ended up in trouble when around many other students, while having success in the restricted area. He wanted to continue with that success. Jim is one of many students who have learned to think for themselves and to make good decisions. Now, children are coming to the supervisors and telling them if others are bothering them. They tell about their problems, and the others are asked the RTP questions. Before, students being bothered would retaliate and get into trouble.

The RTC needs a person who is caring, consistent, and committed: always working to make things better. Ted Huerta, our RTC teacher, is the best person whom I have ever seen at working with children. He deserves much of the credit for our school being RTP certified. I have watched the students run across the playground, heading for the RTC to check in with Ted and show him how well they've succeeded at their plans. They are excited by their progress and are anxious to show him how well they've done, as reflected on their monitoring charts.

The first student in our RTC at the beginning of the 1996–97 school year, James, had transferred from another school, where he had disrupted frequently. He was escorted to the RTC by one of the male teachers. James had been fighting with another student at recess and was in no mood to listen to anybody. He kicked the walls, he cursed, he slammed his fist on the desk, and he had a wild look in his eyes. Ted wisely left him alone after suggesting that if he wanted to talk about what he wanted to do, then he should let Ted know. After a while, James calmed down and said that he would like to talk. It seemed to Ted that James was shocked to learn that he had a choice about what he wanted to do. During that first meeting with James, Ted told him that he couldn't *make* James do *anything*. "Can I make you stop fighting?" Ted asked. "No," James replied. "And is it OK to hurt someone?" Ted continued. "No," James said. To say that James was completely reformed after that encounter with Ted would be an overstatement. There were numerous plans, parent meetings, talks with the counselor, and out-of-school referrals. But underneath all of the anger and tough attitude was a nice, caring boy. He has improved in all areas, and his current referrals to the RTC are rare. He is now on a monitor chart, and Ted sees him every day. James and Ted have developed a good relationship, which I've learned is critical to helping such highly disruptive students. James treats Ted as his surrogate uncle but still has his bad days now and then. Ted says, "In the times when I lose my focus on what the program is about, I re-read one of Ed Ford's little RTP cards, and that says it all. Quoting the card, Ted says, "For children to succeed, they must believe you care about them, that you have confidence in their ability to solve problems, and they must experience mutual respect. The stronger the relationship, the easier it is to resolve differences."

A second grade student who struggled with emotional problems and had a dysfunctional family situation from infancy sought the calm atmosphere of the RTC on those mornings when he felt overwhelmed by circumstances that he couldn't control. Our school provides "chill-out" passes for such situations, allowing students pressure relief and an opportunity for self-control when they realize that they might not be able to "cope" at any given time. After working or relaxing quietly in the RTC for as much time as needed, the student can communicate his or her desire to return to class. This self-imposed removal from class helps the student gain enough confidence to face the rest of the day productively and with composure.

We talk very little about discipline during staff meetings, but we talk a lot about RTP procedures. We used to spend time complaining about how the children were acting. Now, we might spend three minutes role-playing, asking the RTP questions, with teachers trading off the roles of teachers and students.

After a student's third referral to the RTC, a parent conference is held, involving the student, parent(s), teacher(s), counselor, and principal. The parents are wonderful. They know that, through this process, we sincerely want to teach their children responsible thinking skills. It is because of this process that we have formed a partnership with the parents.

During the past three years, Casa Blanca Community School has had approximately 150 parent conferences. They have been extremely helpful, because they have enhanced communication and support between the school and parents. Frequently, when parents are required to attend a meeting with the school administrator and teacher, it is because the student has made a poor choice. A parent might feel embarrassed to receive feedback about his or her student's poor choice, but RTP parent conferences have resulted in improved student choices at school as parents recognize that our genuine concern and caring is aimed only at helping students succeed. The parents and community fully support this program.

When we first began RTP, one parent walked into an RTP meeting and blamed the teacher and school for her son Jimmy hitting another student. She angrily explained how it wasn't his fault for being hurtful to another student. We listened patiently as she vented her thoughts and feelings. The process was then explained by Ted. He focused on how each child is responsible for his or her own choices and said that fighting is not an acceptable choice at Casa Blanca Community School. The teacher then explained the incident, and that, when someone is disturbing a student, the student should let the teacher know. Again, it was emphasized that hitting is not an acceptable choice. The teacher also described some of the student's positive qualities, and the fantastic improvements he had made in reading and math. Another teacher stated that the staff was trying to help the student have a successful school year and to teach him how to make better choices. Our counselor inquired if there were any significant challenges at home that might have been related to Jimmy's hostile response to the other student. Also, she provided support to the parent by acknowledging how much we appreciated her concern in trying to find out exactly what happened. The message being conveyed to the parent was: "We are trying to help your child be successful. With each other's support, we can do this." Slowly, we could see the mother's expression change, and her hostility and anger diminish. Such is often the outcome of RTP parent conferences. Since then, we have had several more RTP conferences with this same parent. She now approaches these conferences in a spirit of cooperation and support. Jimmy's self-esteem has been tremendously enhanced by this program, because he has experienced the wonderful feeling of making choices that result in positive outcomes. He is in control of himself rather than having others control him.

Early in the implementation of RTP, another mother angrily approached an RTP parent conference feeling very agitated. Her attitude was that if the problem occurred at school, then the school should take care of it. The teacher, counselor, and I stressed that we knew her daughter Mary had the ability to be successful at school. With each other's support, this could be accomplished. As in all RTP parent conferences, the counselor inquired about whether there were any issues at home that might be related to what we were seeing at school. At this point, the mother broke down into a stream of tears and sadly told of the recent deaths of several family members. She shared how this had been a difficult time for her and her children. Following this, she was very receptive to suggestions about how she could be of assistance at home with discipline. Again, communication between the school and home provided the extra factor helping Mary to become successful at school.

During the last year and a half, we have observed a significant change in the attitudes of parents/guardians as they approach RTP parent conferences. They are no longer feeling angry with the school, teacher, principal, or even their children. Rather, they are disappointed in the choices that their children have made. They want to work hand-in-hand with the school for the success of their children. One such example is the following. A father came in with his son for an RTP conference. As the conference was in progress, the father conveyed his appreciation for the effort and caring of each of the staff members. He was grateful that the school was using RTP, so that his child, at an early age, could learn to make better choices. He wished that when he was a student, his school had such a process. The wisdom that he spoke brought tears to the eyes of each of the staff members present. All could feel the tremendous amount of love that this father had toward his son. And they could see the student realizing that the adults had faith and confidence in his worth and ability.

In April 1998, nine fourth grade special education students from Casa Blanca Community School enjoyed a six-day trip to Oklahoma City for the Native American Very Special Arts Festival. Before the trip, a meeting was held with students to explain what the trip was all about. Included in the explanation was that, while traveling together, we represented not only ourselves, our families, and our school, but our entire community from the Gila River Indian Reservation. The expectations of how they would respect others were emphasized, and the continuation of RTP during the trip was outlined. It was explained that our usual RTP questions would be asked as needed, and that, if necessary, our school van or one of our hotel rooms would serve as the RTC while a student worked out his or her RTC plan.

Quite frequently along our way, teachers were prompted to ask the RTP questions when students behaved inappropriately. Generally, however, as the first RTP question was asked ("What are you doing?"), students quickly corrected their behaviors. Only in one instance did a student choose to go to the RTC to work out her plan. She had been name-calling and teasing one of the other girls. She was asked all of the RTP questions, and she responded with resolve to not name-call. Shortly thereafter, the girls were dressed to attend a buffet dinner and a Pow-Wow. She resumed name-calling and teasing the same girl as before. When teased by Sue, the girl cried and lost the joy of having a new dress to wear. Sue was told, "I see you have chosen to go to the RTC, which will be in a hotel room, while everyone else attends the buffet dinner and the Pow-Wow. You may work out your plan when you are ready and rejoin the group." Everyone except Sue and one teacher went to dinner. Sue sat in a chair at a table by the window, choosing to stare out the window rather than work on her plan. The sun was setting. The teacher reminded Sue that when she worked out her plan, she could rejoin the group. There was silence. The teacher sat comfortably, reading a book.

Soon, Sue's view through the window was of the dark evening sky. Then there was a knock on the door. One of the other teachers and two students had come bearing dinner, since the buffet line was about to close. The students were anxious to tell the RTC teacher how wonderful the buffet had been, and how excited they were to be going to their first-ever Pow-Wow. The RTC teacher told them to have a good time. Wonderful aromas filled the quiet hotel room, and the teacher proceeded to enjoy some of the delicious dinner. Moments later, a teary-eyed Sue asked for help writing her plan. The teacher's help included listening while Sue verbally sorted out what she had done and developed her plan. The teacher also helped Sue with her spelling as Sue wrote her plan. Sue wrote that she had called the other student "fat," and that she had "broken the rule: keep hands, feet, and name-calling to yourself" (this was her general education teacher's classroom rule). She wrote that she "wanted to be with the group," that she

would not name-call again, that she would "apologize to
the other girl," and that she would "ask the other girl to for-
give her." The teacher and Sue cheerfully finished their dinner, then happily went to rejoin the group. Sue followed
through on her plan to apologize to the other girl and to
ask for forgiveness. The girls sealed the plan with a hug. Sue
did not name-call again; in fact, after the RTC episode, there
were no further incidents requiring development of a plan
for the remainder of the trip. Through using RTP, the dig-
nity of all parties was respected, we all grew a little, and we
all enjoyed an outstanding trip!

The successful implementation of RTP requires a team
approach by the entire staff. Our counselor, Harriet West, is
a key person in our program. As already noted, parents frequently feel defensive or angry at first when they attend
meetings that address poor choices their children have
made, and Harriet has a very unique quality that helps parents feel more comfortable when discussing their children's behavior. She is the best counselor I have ever seen.
When she acknowledges how parents might be feeling
regarding their children's choices, it helps to reduce the
distance between the parents and the school. At the same
time, she is able to tactfully seek information about home
situations that might be related to poor choices made at
school by the students. And she often provides the opportunity to meet privately with parents following RTP conferences, so that further exploration of home situations can be
examined. Harriet exhibits much warmth and caring to-
wards our parents. This results in openness of parents to
work with the school.

The administrator's role in the RTP program is very
demanding, yet very rewarding. This is a program that cannot be administered from an office chair. The administrator needs to be actively modeling the principles everywhere on campus. For three years, I have been learning and
modeling the program.

The questioning process is probably the hardest aspect
of RTP for the administrator, as well as for the rest of the

staff. At first, the questioning process involves learning all seven questions. This might seem easy, but our staff experienced difficulty in mastering the questions. Sometimes we forgot to ask the questions. Eventually, for the students who have learned the process well, only the first and last questions are critical. Role-playing helped most. I had the staff role-play at every staff meeting for 10 minutes the first year; now, in our third year, we role-play for two to three minutes at each meeting. New staff and new kindergarten students each year need the same training. It took nearly one and a half years before I felt like we were making an "A" in the questioning process: 98 percent of the teachers were asking the questions correctly and asking the questions 98 percent of the time. After one and a half years, Ted Huerta still randomly asks the children coming to the RTC if the teacher asked them the questions before they chose to go to the RTC. We don't want teachers using the process if they're not using it correctly.

We also continue to work on RTP procedures: for example, sending a written referral with the student when he or she disrupts the second time and chooses to go to the RTC. It required about a year and a half to obtain consistency on this. If a student chose to go to the RTC and didn't receive a written referral, then the student was sent back to the referring teacher. On one occasion when I was in the RTC and a student walked in without a referral, I asked the student who had sent her. I called on the phone and told the teacher that the child was returning, and that she must have a written referral before leaving the classroom. At first, the teacher was not very happy with me, but we now remember the procedure. It takes a lot of practice to refine this written referral procedure.

As you can see, this is a school-wide program, with a *team* approach. Everything we do is a team effort. What do we get out of that team effort? The greatest staff, the greatest parents, and the greatest children.

Chapter 18
RTP and the
Probation Officer

Jake Jacobs
Deputy Adult Probation Officer III
Maricopa County, Arizona

Jake has been a close friend for over 20 years, and I've worked to help him incorporate RTP into his probation work. In a punitive, coercive system such as corrections, it might seem strange that RTP could be so effective. But it is. Rather than being in school, the probationer is in the custody of the court. As in school, the purpose of RTP is to help the probationer learn to take responsibility for his own life, while learning how to respect the rights of others. The probation officer acts as both RTC teacher and administrator. His job is to teach his probationers how to think for themselves, how to learn the skills to make successful plans, and how to keep from being incarcerated. In schools, when students continue to disrupt, they have chosen to go home; in probation work, they have chosen to be incarcerated. The rules, called terms and conditions, are set by a judge.

A particularly interesting phenomenon is that Jake's probationers rarely get upset with him. They feel respected. Even those whose probation has been revoked by Jake have rarely gotten angry with him. In fact, several of them have sent him letters while incarcerated, and some have contacted him again when they got out of prison.—Ed Ford

"Hi, You've reached Jake Jacobs, your friendly Probation Officer of the Adult Probation and Youthful Offender Program, where I jump-start your life!" By using RTP, I *do* help to "jump-start" the lives of those assigned to me. I've had over 16 years experience in Adult Probation in Maricopa County, which covers the greater metropolitan area of Phoenix. This includes five years with the youthful offender program.

Persons who have been convicted of breaking the law and are sentenced to probation are called probationers. Their sentences are specific in length and have explicit terms and conditions that must be met during that time. These terms and conditions are mandated by a Criminal Court judge in the Superior Court. Probationers are monitored by probation officers (commonly referred to as PO's), who ensure compliance with the terms and conditions of probation.

A typical case is that of a person convicted of burglary, underlying which is a problem related to substance abuse. The person might receive a sentence of five years on probation with fines and restitution to be paid, a defined number of hours of community service work to be completed, and a requirement for getting treatment for substance abuse.

The criminal justice system is punitive and very threatening. Probation means that the convicted person remains free in the community (under the supervision of the PO) as long as all of the terms and conditions of probation are met. Otherwise, probation could be revoked, with the person being sentenced to jail or prison. The system is intimidating! PO's are usually viewed as strict authoritarians by their probationers. Yet nearly all of my probationers see me as caring and non-punitive. How can that be? What makes what I do so different that I am looked at as someone who makes a difference in probationers' lives, shows respect and concern for their futures, and helps them formulate plans enabling them to build the necessary confidence to become successful? It is simply that I have taken RTP to heart and apply it in my job every day.

For many years, Ed Ford and I have conducted a series of

group sessions with probationers to encourage and teach them how to think, and to help them develop skills allowing them to deal more effectively with their lives. The foundation for my work with probationers comes from two questions Ed has taught me to always keep in mind:

Who does the thinking when you tell?

Who does the thinking when you ask?

To help probationers change their life styles, probation officers must help them learn how to think responsibly for themselves and how to respect the rights of others. How can this be done? By asking questions. It's that simple. Telling probationers what to do just does not work, just as it does not work in other situations: parents try to tell their children what to do, and the children leave home; teachers try to tell their students what to do, and the students leave school; the policeman yells, "Stop or I'll shoot!" and the suspect keeps running, possibly getting shot.

Over the years, I have overheard many PO's lecturing their clients—sometimes screaming at them, pleading with them, and threatening them. I have seen PO's become upset when their probationers don't follow the terms and conditions. These PO's have taken on the non-compliance of the probationers as their own problem. But I use RTP. My attitude is based in part on a question posed by my friend, Ernie Garcia, who was Director of the Juvenile Court Services in Maricopa County for over 20 years: "Whose problem is it?" Non-compliance is a problem that belongs to the probationer, not to the probation officer.

RTP works well for me because my probationers think about what they are doing and look at the quality of the lives they are living. Without RTP, probationers often use their past as an excuse. "I really don't belong here. It was my buddy who talked me into it. I'm innocent." "It's my ex-wife's fault." "Those old folks shouldn't have left their door open for me." I often ask those convicted of burglary:

"Shouldn't you change your profession? If you were any good at what you've been doing, I wouldn't have met you."

In schools, the second RTP question is "What are the rules?" In probation, that question becomes "What are the terms and conditions?" These are the rules for each probationer. And just as the responsible thinking classroom gives students help in school, the probation office becomes the RTC for probationers. If students choose to continue to disrupt and not follow the rules in the RTC, they go home. If probationers choose to continue to break the law or not abide by their terms and conditions, they go to jail or prison. I am not the one who causes them to be imprisoned, and I do not threaten them with it. But I must work within the criminal justice system while assisting my probationers to succeed by avoiding incarceration. It is their life style choice that has brought them to me, and it is their choice that will lead them either to follow the rules set by a judge or to break those rules and go to a penal institution.

Like a teacher using RTP, I attempt to find out what probationers want to do. If they want help in changing, I'll help. If, by their actions, they exhibit a desire to go to jail, that's no problem for me, because I consider it their decision. I am always willing to work with them when they are truly committed. I just keep asking questions.

Probationers usually are in conflict with others and not in control of their lives. They have a hard time starting and finishing a program or project. Therefore, when working with probationers, it's important to be specific. They need to learn how to set goals and standards. The PO must stay "in the here and now," keep them focused, teach them how to make a plan, and get genuine commitment to follow that plan. To do these things, ask questions. Asking questions centers both the PO and the probationer on the real and present issues before them.

By way of illustration, the following is a typical exchange with a probationer, whom I'll call Don. Don comes into my office after I have received a report that he had a dirty urine test. This means that Don violated his terms and conditions of probation by having a positive drug test result, indicating use of cocaine.

Jake: So, how have things been going, Don? Are you staying clean and sober?

Don: Sure, I'm doin' OK. So, how are you doin', Jake?

Jake: What are you doing about your sobriety? Are you staying clean and sober? (Focusing on the issue at hand.)

Don: I need to be honest and tell you that I had a relapse last week.

Jake: Is the issue honesty or sobriety? (Again, staying focused.)

Don: Have you ever done drugs? (Trying to change the subject.)

Jake: What do your terms say about drug use? (Keeping him focused.)

Don: You don't want to help me. You just want to send me to prison. (Trying to shift the blame.)

Jake: What do your terms say about drug use? (Still staying focused.)

Don: I have to stay clean and sober.

Jake: What happens if you don't stay clean and sober on probation?

Don: I'll go back to jail.

Jake: Do you think I want to send you back to jail?

Don: No, I guess not. But can you give me a break?

Jake: Do you think I shouldn't follow what the judge directed? (Keeping attention on the terms and conditions.)

Don: No, I guess not.

Jake: Would I be the one who sends you back to jail?

Don: No, I guess I would be doing it to myself.

Jake: How would you send yourself to jail?

Don: Yeah, I know. By doing drugs. Violating terms.

Jake: So, what are your choices? What do you want to do?

Don: What do you mean?

Jake: Do you want treatment or jail?

Don: I guess I need help.

Jake: Do you want residential treatment or residential jail?

Don: I want treatment.

Jake: Do you want to work at this or not? (Testing for commitment.)

Don: Yeah. I guess so. (A weak commitment.)

Jake: Are you sure? If you want your probation revoked, that's fine by me. (Still testing.)

Don: No, No. I don't want to go back to jail. No. I'll stay clean. I promise. I really will.

Jake: So, what's your plan to stay clean and sober?

Don: I've been thinking maybe I should try AA.

Jake: What are your terms and conditions?

Don: I have to attend meetings or be in a residential program.

Jake: So, what's your plan?

Don: Boy, you don't let up, do you?

Jake: Do you want me to let up?

Don: No. No! I've got to do this. Well, there's an AA meeting tonight at the Garfield Center. I'll be there.

Jake: How will I know?

Don: I guess you have to trust me.

Jake: How will I know you've attended the meeting?

Don: I'll have the guy running the meeting call you.

Jake: What if he doesn't call me?

Don: OK, so I'll call you with his name and phone number. How's that?

Jake: What about your sponsor's name and phone number?

Don: OK, OK, I'll call that in as well. But what if I forget to call?

Jake: What's my alternative?

Don: I'll call. I'll call. I really will.

Jake: When?

Don: I'll call tomorrow morning, and if you aren't there, I'll leave the message on your answering machine. Is that OK?

Jake: What do you think?

Don: That'll work. I'll be in touch tomorrow.

This is an example of an exchange with a probationer

who wants to avoid the issue of his sobriety. Telling Don what to do or lecturing him only helps the PO feel better. It does *not* get Don to think about improving the quality of his life, or to concentrate on the standards he must maintain to keep his freedom. If I don't teach Don to think responsibly on his own, when I'm not around, he is going to go back to using drugs. Teaching him to think by asking him questions really works. And asking questions and being sure I get answers make my job much easier. It's actually fun. I watch the probationers struggle, but I also watch them succeed. I see them improve their family life and begin to secure better jobs. I observe them taking control of their lives. When I ask questions and respect the answers, the probationers sense that respect. For the first time for many of them, they experience being respected. Then they learn from that experience to show respect for others. Their correctional careers have been filled with yelling and telling, lecturing and more lecturing. None of that has taught them to think. It has locked them further into their own inadequate lives.

By asking questions, I teach probationers to *think* whenever they are tempted to use alcohol or drugs, to drive on a suspended license, or to skip work that day. I just keep asking what they have been doing and what are the consequences of their actions. It takes the pressure off me. I don't feel any more guilty when probationers choose to be incarcerated than a teacher or administrator feels when students who continue to disrupt choose to go home.

Asking questions in a calm, respectful, and curious voice develops rapport with probationers. This has frequently created relationships with me that continue long after release from probation. I still hear from many probationers after I have stopped supervising them. Even some probationers who had their probations revoked and were incarcerated have sent me friendly letters from prison. I always wanted a pen pal, and now I have pals in the pen! Their letters thank me for my support and for helping them to think about the standards they need to set for themselves to become more successful. I have never received an angry letter or one that blamed me for what happened.

It is most important to ask the right kind of questions. I never ask "why" because the response will inevitably be filled with excuses. Asking the right questions has allowed me to avoid all of the garbage, so I can focus on the major issues for each probationer.

Ed Ford has taught me about commitment. If you don't have commitment to what you do, you don't have anything. This applies to your personal life, your marriage, your job, your health, and your happiness. For probationers, it's not merely talking about trying to get a job, or trying to stay clean and sober. It's a commitment to change what hasn't worked in the past, to make things work now, and to improve the standard of their lives. It's a commitment to change how they want to perceive themselves.

When I begin to feel angry or upset with a probationer, I ask myself Ernie Garcia's question: "Whose problem is it?" If a plan isn't being adhered to, I go back and test for commitment. If I am working harder than a probationer to keep him out of jail, then I am doing something wrong. I return to the plan with the probationer and test for commitment. I just start asking more questions.

Have I chosen to love my work? Yes. Have I chosen to love RTP? Yes!

Many thanks to my wife, Patricia, and to my good friend, Judge C. Kimball Rose, retired.

Part 4. Understanding the Differences

Chapter 19
Perceptual Control Theory, Reality Therapy, and the Responsible Thinking Process

W. Thomas Bourbon, Ph.D.
Perceptual Control Theorist
Rochelle, Texas

with extensive help from
Caroline Bourbon Young

and assistance from
Tim Carey

The relationship of RTP and PCT to William Glasser's ideas have been misconstrued by some educators over a period of several years. I am pleased that this chapter sets the record straight with abundant documentary evidence.
—Ed Ford

In his Responsible Thinking Process (RTP) for schools, Ed Ford tries to apply principles from a unique science of behavior, perceptual control theory (PCT), developed by William T. Powers. When they first hear about RTP, many people think that it is the same as one of the various school programs developed by William Glasser, and they think PCT is identical to some ideas that Glasser used to call Control Theory (CT). I believe that those people are wrong: RTP is unlike anything Glasser allows to occur in schools, and PCT is a formal science, whereas Glasser's ideas about his Control Theory are unscientific personal speculations.

Why are so many people confused about the relationships between Ford, Powers, and Glasser? Why do so many
people think programs and ideas that are different from
one another are identical? In this chapter, I explain simi-
larities and differences between RTP and Glasser's various
programs, and I briefly describe the history of interactions
between Powers, Glasser, and Ford. After you read this
chapter, you can decide for yourself whether Ford's RTP
and Glasser's programs are the same, and whether the science of PCT is identical to Glasser's speculations.

Some Initial Comparisons

Ford's RTP and Powers's PCT: In RTP, Ed Ford says that
teachers are responsible for teaching their subjects, and for
using simple questions and making referrals to the responsible thinking classroom (RTC) whenever students disrupt.
Ford also says that students are responsible for not disturbing others unnecessarily, whether they are teachers engaged in instruction or other students engaged in studying
and learning. A student who continues to disrupt is referred to the RTC to develop a plan for how he will avoid
disrupting in situations like the one where he disrupted
before. Adults and students are responsible for the consequences of their own actions, and not for the actions of any
other person.

When Ford designed RTP, he had in mind a specific mathematical theory of behavior: perceptual control theory, as
developed by Powers and his colleagues beginning in the
1950s. Since 1981, Ford has worked to better understand
PCT and to modify his clinical practices, bringing them into
closer agreement with principles from the science. (Ford's
RTP is *not* PCT; rather, RTP is his attempt to *apply* principles from PCT.) In PCT, Powers says a person decides that
some of his own perceptions should be a certain way, and
then he acts to make them be the way that he intends. The
person's actions are understood to be the uncontrolled, or
variable, means to a specific end: controlled perceptions.

PCT scientists recognize that people do not always try to control the same perceptions—sometimes people control remarkably different perceptions. Furthermore, a person is often unaware of the details of her own actions that control her own perceptions, and she is often unaware that her actions disturb other people.

Ford's RTP is designed to help students and teachers control their own perceptions, in school, without unnecessarily disturbing other people. When one person does disturb someone else, perhaps unavoidably or unknowingly, RTP provides a way to deal with the disturbance in a way that minimizes conflict. In schools where RTP is used well, teachers and students are equally likely to say that their lives have changed for the better. The procedures in RTP, and some of the basic principles of PCT, are described in more detail throughout this book and in *Discipline for Home and School, Book One*.

Cause-effect theories of behavior: In nearly every theory of behavior other than PCT, a person's behavior is said to be the end result (effect) of previous events (causes). In cause-effect (C-E) theories, the prior causes of a person's actions are said to reside in places like the environment; or the person's family history and social history; or the person's mind; or brain chemistry; or genes. The list of possible locations for the alleged "causes" is almost endless. Most often, people who use C-E theories to design clinical or disciplinary interventions say that a person is not responsible for his actions or for their consequences. Instead, responsibility resides in the place that is alleged to cause the actions: in the environment; in the person's family history; in the person's brain chemistry; in the person's genes; in inherited "drives" or "needs"; and so on. Not surprisingly, applications of C-E principles in clinics and schools usually hold one person or group of people responsible for another person's actions and their consequences. For example, if a student, Sally, disrupts a school classroom, a teacher, Mr. Amos, is held accountable for Sally's disruption, under the idea that Mr. Amos had created an environment that caused Sally to disrupt. Had Mr. Amos created the proper environment, it would have caused Sally to behave without disruption to others.

If the explanation of behavior in PCT science is correct, then all C-E theories of behavior are wrong. Behavior is not an end result or effect, caused by forces that operate elsewhere. Behavior is the variable means by which a person controls some of her own perceptions.

Glasser's ideas about cause-effect: From the 1960s until now, William Glasser has created a series of programs for schools incorporating features from his Reality Therapy (RT). Glasser designed RT, and all of his school programs, around a traditional cause-effect theory that he used to call Control Theory but now calls Choice Theory (still CT). He says that a person chooses all of her behavior to satisfy a fixed number of inherited "needs" that all people have in common. The number of the alleged "needs" identified by Glasser has varied from two in 1965 to four or five (or maybe five or six) as I write this chapter in early 1999. But that is of little importance; no scientific evidence supports a claim that all people share *any* number of needs.

Glasser's C-E theory of behavior leads to a natural conclusion that, if a student disrupts in school, the environment of the school was the cause. Had the adults in the school created an environment that met all of the student's needs, then she would not have disrupted. In other words, had Mr. Amos met all of Sally's needs, then she would not have disrupted his class. Glasser says that disruptions cease when a teacher "does Choice Theory" in the classroom. (Glasser often writes about "doing" Choice Theory. Whenever he does that, he fails to distinguish between his theory, which is supposed to be an explanation of facts, and its application, in the form of whatever is his current discipline program for schools.)

I do not think Glasser intends for CT to include ideas of traditional cause-effect. In all of his writings, he says that his ideas are different from stimulus-response (S-R) theory, which is the most widely recognized version of C-E theory.

But in spite of what Glasser says about S-R theory, in CT, his explanations of behavior clearly depend on principles of cause-effect that are identical to the ones used in S-R psychology. All Glasser has done is to move the alleged causes from the environment to somewhere inside the person, where a majority of contemporary psychologists and brain scientists have also moved them. Glasser says that behavior is internally motivated, but he also says that environmental conditions are responsible for behavior. Perhaps I am wrong, but it is my impression that Glasser's message to educators is that Sally's behavior is "driven" by her inborn "needs," but when he fails to meet Sally's needs, Mr. Amos is responsible for her misbehavior, while Sally always controls her own "total behavior." (Later in this chapter, I cite examples of the many places where Glasser says these contradictory things.) While Glasser says that Sally controls her own behavior, he also rejects the idea that she uses her behavior to control her own perceptions.

You tell me: I see significant differences between the ideas of Powers and Ford, on the one hand, and those of Glasser, on the other. Unlike me, many people think that there is no difference at all between Ed Ford's Responsible Thinking Process and William Glasser's Reality Therapy and Quality Schools. Many of the same people think that Bill Powers's perceptual control theory is identical to something that Glasser used to call Control Theory. In the rest of this chapter, I describe some of the differences between Powers's ideas and Glasser's, and between Ford's RTP and Glasser's programs. I also describe some of the ways in which Powers, Ford, and Glasser have interacted. After you read my accounts, *you* tell *me* whether Glasser's ideas are identical to Powers's and Ford's.

A Simple Mental Exercise

Too hot, too cold, just right: For a few minutes, forget about all of the things I discussed in the above paragraphs. Imagine that you are alone in a large room equipped with a thermostat and an air-conditioning system. If you think that the temperature of the room feels "too hot" or "too cold," you will adjust the thermostat until the air conditioner changes the temperature, and the room feels "just right" to you. By the way, that is what PCT is all about: the ways that you use your actions to make your perceptions of something (in this case "degree of coolness or warmth") be just right for you.

Now suppose that one other person joins you in the room. Will that person necessarily agree that the temperature feels "just right?" Not necessarily. What will happen if the two of you disagree? Keep that question in mind while you continue to read. We will return to it later.

Mission impossible: Now imagine that 100 people join you in the room. The thermostat is set to the temperature that felt "just right" to you when you were alone. How likely is it that the room will feel "just right" to all 100 people, simultaneously? Could you ever change the temperature of the room to make it feel "just right" to 100 people, simultaneously? Of course not. When the room feels "just right" to some people, it will simultaneously feel "too hot" or "too cold" to some other people. "Too hot," "too cold," and "just right" are not objective physical conditions of the room, on which we can all agree; they are perceptions in the minds of people in the room, and different people have different perceptions of the same physical condition.

In this example, we are considering a simple perception directly related to a physiological state that each of us controls. Each of us feels "too hot," "too cold," or "just right," depending on the temperature of our skin, relative to the core temperature of our body. In humans, core temperature is controlled by a neural system in the brainstem, and the temperature of the air around us affects the temperature of our skin. Left to ourselves, each of us would create a different temperature of the room and declare that the condition that satisfies us individually is "just right." There is no physical temperature that can satisfy all of us at the same time.

Now imagine that you are told by a person who evaluates your performance that you must keep the 100 people in the room comfortable—all of them at the same time. If even one of the 100 people thinks the room is "too hot" or "too cold," the evaluator says that you have failed as a professional person, and you will be penalized. Is that fair? If there are only 50 people in the room, is it fair? Does it matter if there are only 20 or 30 people?

Is it possible for one person to alter the environment so as to make the perceptions of temperature be "just right" for all other people, simultaneously? Is it possible for one person to adjust *any* aspect of the environment so that it satisfies all other people, simultaneously? Is it reasonable to expect Mr. Amos to accomplish such an impossible task? Is it fair to tell him that he has "failed" and, as a consequence of his failure, he is responsible for the subsequent behavior of all of the other people, including Sally? You tell me.

The remainder of this chapter has four parts: first, a brief history of Powers's perceptual control theory, Glasser's Reality Therapy, and the relationship between them; second, a comparison of Powers's PCT and Glasser's Control Theory; third, a chronology of PCT, Ed Ford's work, and Glasser's Reality Therapy and Control Theory; and fourth, a comparison of RTP and Glasser's Quality Schools and Choice Theory.

A Brief History of PCT and RT/CT

Powers and PCT: Historically, William T. Powers and PCT come before both William Glasser and his ideas, and Ed Ford and his RTP. In the early 1950s, Powers made the brilliant observation that people act to control many, but not all, of their own perceptions. A person who controls her perceptions must act to affect parts of the world. From our vantage point outside the person, we see events and relationships and processes in her world that would otherwise *vary*, but that she *controls*, which is to say that she keeps them at some predetermined states or conditions. Many factors affect the temperature of the air in a room and cause it to vary. However, a person uses the thermostat to affect the air-conditioner, which keeps the air in the room at a temperature that feels "just right" to her, no matter what else, including other people, might cause the temperature of the air to change. A car hurtling along the road at high speed would soon end up in a ditch, or against a tree, or crashing into another car, except for the driver's actions. The driver keeps the car moving toward the destination he selects, along the route he selects, at the speed he selects, in the lane he selects, at his selected distance behind a car ahead. Think about all of the perceptions a driver controls while driving from one destination to another, and think about how different the events that we observers see in the world would be if the driver were not controlling those perceptions.

To explain how people control their perceptions, Powers developed control system theory (CST), which was the early name for what is now called perceptual control theory. The current name was adopted early in the 1990s to distinguish Powers's theory from many incorrect ideas that some people had begun to call "control theory." Glasser's Control Theory (now called Choice Theory) is of those incorrect versions.

In a nutshell, Powers says that *people do not plan or control their actions, which most behavioral scientists call their behavior. Instead, they act, in any way necessary, to eliminate, or prevent, differences between actual and intended perceptions. As observers, we see the person's actions, but we are often unaware of what the person is really doing; we are unaware of the perceptions that the person is controlling by way of the actions we see.* (Much of Powers's earlier writing is available in two collections: *Living Control Systems I* (previously published papers), 1989; and *Living Control Systems II* (previously unpublished papers), 1992. Both books are available from Benchmark Publications, New Canaan, Connecticut.)

In 1973, more than 20 years after he began his work on PCT, Powers published a book, *Behavior: The Control of Perception* (*BCP*), and a companion article, "Feedback: Beyond Behaviorism," in the journal *Science*. (*BCP* was published by Aldine, in Chicago; it is currently available from Benchmark Publications.) In 1973, I read those two publications. Immediately, I saw that Powers had resolved many of the terrible fallacies I knew existed in traditional psychology. I became part of a small group of behavioral scientists working to develop PCT through behavioral research and computer modeling.

PCT is a mathematical theory of behavior, and it is radically different from any major traditional theory in the behavioral, social, or cognitive sciences, or in the brain sciences and life sciences. At the core of PCT is a *testable* model of behavior, not just a system of ideas that Powers *believes*. When we do PCT science the way we should, any time we think that there is a way to change the theory to make it better, we test the change to see if it produces the expected results. If it does not, then we must reject the change, no matter how much we like it. We accept proposed changes to the basic PCT model only if they improve the way the model works.

Glasser and RT/CT: William Glasser is a psychiatrist, an M.D. In 1965, he published a book in which he described his Reality Therapy. For many years, I taught about RT as one of many kinds of psychiatric therapy. I always thought that RT was more sensible and humane than many of the other therapies. It belongs in the group of therapies that are present-centered, rather than centered on events in the client's past. Present-centered therapists treat a client as an active agent, capable of changing the course of her own life.

William Glasser is a psychiatrist, not a research scientist, even though as a very young man he did study chemical engineering. Those are facts, not criticism. In the 1960s, Glasser had no scientific explanation for RT. Eventually, he discovered Powers's 1973 publications about CST. He asked Powers to explain CST to him, and he decided that CST explained RT. In 1981, Glasser published his book *Stations of the Mind*. It included a Foreword by Powers. In the book, Glasser introduced his own version of what he called Control Theory. It bore only slight resemblance to Powers's theory. In 1984, Glasser published a book called *Control Theory*. From then until 1996, Control Theory was prominent in most of his writings and in the name of his institute. During that time, Glasser claimed he had developed CT and improved it far beyond what Powers had done. *Glasser's claim is not justified for scientific control theory.* Glasser's misappropriation and misuse of Powers's name has led to decades of confusion in which many people innocently believed, because the names of Glasser's speculations and Powers's scientific theory were similar, that the sets of ideas were the same. That conclusion is absolutely incorrect.

I think Glasser never realized that his Control Theory was merely a non-functional verbal statement of his own beliefs about behavior. Glasser's CT was not, in any way, a formal, testable, scientific theory of behavior. It was never intended to be such a theory. In fact, when we organize a formal model of behavior according to the principles that Glasser describes, the model cannot function in anything like the way Glasser believes it does. To the degree that Reality Therapy works in psychiatry and the Quality School program works in schools, they *cannot* work solely for the reasons that Glasser stated in his Control Theory. For example, as an aid to understanding how his CT explains therapy, Glasser, like PCT scientists, uses the example of a person driving a car. PCT scientists model the successful driver as a person who has learned which perceptions to control, by means of any actions that are necessary, but I believe Glasser would say that the driver is successful because she learned to select and control her behavior, so that she makes the "real world" match a "picture in her mind." Which of the two explanations, Powers's PCT, or Glasser's CT, can tell us how a person successfully drives her car on a long trip, in spite of countless unexpected events that occur along the way? You tell me.

A Comparison of PCT and CT/RT

Above, I summarized the history of PCT, and I described how William Glasser began to use a nonfunctional version of PCT to explain his popular and effective Reality Therapy. I also made a brief comparison between PCT and Glasser's ideas. Now I make a more detailed comparison between the ideas. Later I will show some implications of those differences, as they play out in Ford's and Glasser's approaches to working with students.

There have always been many issues to address when comparing Powers's and Glasser's ideas, but the task was made even more difficult in 1996, when Glasser decreed that, in all of his earlier writings where he had used the term Control Theory, readers were to substitute the term Choice Theory. In the present comparison, I quote from Glasser's Introduction to "Programs, Policies & Procedures of the William Glasser Institute," distributed in September 1996. In doing so, I have honored Glasser's request and substituted Choice Theory for Control Theory. I apologize for any confusion caused by this, but it is as Glasser wants. Following quotes from Glasser, I contrast what he says with ideas in PCT.

Definitions of "Behavior"

Glasser: "Choice Theory attempts to explain both the psychological and physiological behavior of all living creatures. In Choice Theory, these two aspects of behavior are combined and called, *Total Behavior*."

"This theory maintains that all we do from birth to death is behave, and all of our behavior is Total Behavior. Total Behavior is made up of four components, *acting*, *thinking*, *feeling* and the *physiology*, which always accompanies the other three components."

Bourbon: There is nothing new to the idea that, in humans, processes like those Glasser identifies as thinking, acting, feeling, and physiology occur together. Even many die-hard radical behaviorists would agree with that idea. B. F. Skinner certainly said similar things. The familiar idea that many things are going on at the same time is not unique to Glasser's thinking.

Remember, Glasser said that his CT is supposed to explain the behavior of all living creatures. I cannot imagine what kind of evidence he might use to support the idea that slugs, bacteria, and amoebae always act, think, and feel, along with their physiology. This is not a trivial matter: either the terms that Glasser invokes are part of a scientific theory that explains the behavior of all living things, or they are not. Which is the case?

PCT theorists intend for PCT to explain the behavior of all living things. In PCT, what most scientists call *behavior* is identified as the observed *actions* of a living thing. The actions are the means by which the living system controls its perceptions, however simple they might be, of the states of certain variables in the world. In PCT, we do not assume that every action is accompanied by subjective states of thinking and feeling. In the formal mathematical model for PCT, there are only "signals" that can vary in magnitude and "functions" that receive input signals and compute output signals. In the formal model, there is no necessity to assume that all perceptions reach "conscious" subjective awareness, although it is obvious that many human perceptions reach that level. In a bacterium like *Escherichia coli*, there are internal chemical "signals" proportional to the concentrations of various substances in the environment. It looks like *E. coli* acts to control the magnitudes of those signals, making some increase and others decrease. In PCT, we treat those chemical signals like perceptions, and we use the same basic model to explain how *E. coli* controls those simple perceptions as well as to explain how a person controls her subjective experiences of the loudness of a radio or the size of her bank account.

"Choice" of Behavior

Glasser: "Choice Theory explains that all Total Behavior is chosen and all the choices are an ongoing attempt to change the *real world* so that it coincides with a small, simulated world that we build into our memory called the *Quality World*."

Bourbon: First, in PCT we recognize that living things do not choose their behavioral actions. Rather, they choose which perceptions should occur, then their actions vary in any ways necessary to create the selected perceptions, and to defend them against changes that might otherwise be produced by independent disturbances from the environment. We have demonstrated that a system that selects its actions in advance cannot possibly select and control any intended consequences of its actions. Consider a person driving a car. Can the driver select, before the fact of driving over a particular stretch of road, the specific movements of his hands and feet that will be needed to manipulate the steering wheel, the gas pedal, and other devices in the car? Of course not. It is impossible to drive that way, unless, of course, one is deliberately courting disaster. Instead, the driver decides in advance on which perceptions will occur —perceptions of the route, speed, acceptable proximity to other cars, and other aspects of the trip—and then acts as needed to create and defend those intended perceptions.

Second, an organism does not directly perceive "the real world." All that an organism experiences directly are its own perceptions. PCT uses models that portray living systems as acting to control some of their own perceptions, often by acting on the external world. But an organism "knows" the world only as perceptions, not as something that is independent of perceptions and more real than they are. Among perceptual control theorists, a favorite saying used to summarize our ideas about behavior is "It's all perception."

This brings us to a summary of some clear differences between Glasser's ideas and those in PCT. Glasser says that

Alfredo selects his behaviors so as to make the real world match Alfredo's "picture" of what the real world should be. In PCT, we say that Alfredo acts, any way necessary as demanded by immediate circumstances, to make his perceptions of the world match the perceptions he intends. If Alfredo is to control his perceptions, he cannot select his actions; they must be free to vary. In the document from which I quoted, Glasser would require, first, that Alfredo know the world just as it is, and second, that Alfredo select in advance the actions that will make the real world match his pictures of an ideal world. PCT requires, first, that Alfredo decide which perceptions he will have of some part of the world, and then, if there is a discrepancy between what he intends to perceive and what he does perceive, he acts, in any way that is sufficient to eliminate the discrepancy. PCT does not require that Alfredo directly perceive the "real world." Which assumption do you think is the most reasonable, Glasser's or Powers's?

"Needs"

Glasser: The "Quality World" is built "starting shortly after birth, from all we have perceived that feels very good. What feels very good is anything we do that satisfies, or in the case of addictions, seems to satisfy, one or more of *five basic needs built into our genetic structure: survival, love, belonging, power, freedom and fun.*"

Bourbon: The subject of "needs" provides one of the clearest differences between scientific PCT and Glasser's personal opinions about behavior. The idea that organisms are born with a fixed set of "needs," serving to motivate or energize their behavior, has a long, troublesome history in philosophy and psychology. Theorists have often claimed that needs are products of our nature, genes, anatomy, and physiology, or some other internal predisposing factor. They have claimed that we have needs numbering between one and many dozens. When they say there is one, it is usually called a "need for survival." When there are dozens . . .

I won't bother you with that. When there are five, they might be, or might not be, assigned the same names that Glasser uses. *When it comes to "needs," any guess is as good as any other. There is no scientific reason to choose one list of needs over any other list, or to rely on the idea of needs at all.*

From the beginnings of RT, Glasser has insisted that all people share the same needs, and that those needs motivate our behavior. Even many professional people who have broken away from Glasser over fundamental issues still cling fiercely to his idea of needs. In contrast to Glasser and his followers, perceptual control theorists see no evidence for the presence or importance of a fixed set of needs. How do we resolve this disagreement? I know only one way out. One of my areas of specialization as a student and professor was the history of science, in particular, the history of psychology. Let me tell you just a little about the many different ways the idea of needs has been used in behavioral science. After you see what I say, you tell me if there is any scientific reason to accept any person's list of alleged "needs."

A short history of "needs" in behavioral science: The idea that people behave to satisfy certain needs became part of modern science largely through the work of Charles Darwin in the 19th century. Darwin used the ancient idea of "instinct" to explain animal behavior. He said behavior is one of the features by which "natural selection" determines which individuals live and which die. Darwin called instincts the internal driving and steering forces in animal behavior; he said that instincts motivate or energize behavior, and that they guide behavior in particular directions. Following Darwin's publications on evolution, the idea that instincts motivate and direct behavior became popular among psychologists. In 1892, the great American psychologist William James used instincts as part of his explanation of human behavior.

In 1908, William McDougall described 12 "instincts" that motivate and direct behavior. By 1932, he changed the list to between 14 and 18 "propensities." (As you will see, the names and numbers of these alleged "internal motivators" change with the wind!) In 1915, Sigmund Freud wrote that internal instincts or "drives" are the main motivators of behavior. At first, Freud said that there are two groups of motivators, one for self-preservation and the other for sexual matters. Later, Freud said that there is only one internal influence, the libido; later still, he again said that there are two, the life instinct and the death instinct. (More of those easy changes.)

In 1922, Kurt Lewin said that behavior is internally motivated by a set of "determining tendencies," but by 1928, they had become a set of "needs," divided into "biological needs" and "quasi [psychological?] needs." In 1932, P. T. Young wrote about 17 "primary drives." In 1938, Henry A. Murray defined needs this way: "A need is a construct (a convenient fiction or hypothetical concept) which stands for a force (the physico-chemical nature of which is unknown) in the brain region, a force which organizes perception, apperception, intellection, conation, and action in such a way as to transform in a certain direction an existing unsatisfactory situation. . . . each need is characteristically accompanied by a particular feeling or emotion . . ." Murray listed approximately *40* needs: 13 he called "viscerogenic" (physiological?), and the remainder were called "psychogenic." By 1951, Murray changed the term "need" to "thematic disposition."

Are you confused by now? I am. You see, once a scientist says that all behavior is energized and guided by a set of common internal causes shared by all people, there is no limit (upper *or* lower) on the number of causes the scientist can imagine, or on the names the scientist gives to them. It is all a matter of aesthetics, preferences, and personal biases. It is not a matter of science. By the time we reach Murray in our tour of history, there are shelves filled with research articles, graduate theses, and books on subjects like Freud's instincts (two, one, or a different two), Young's 17 primary drives, and Murray's 40 needs (and his later similar number of thematic dispositions). There is no scientific way to decide which of these alternatives is correct. Young was right when he said that none of these "things" exist, except as convenient fictions. Let's look quickly at a few more fictions.

In 1959, R. B. Cattell wrote about 16 "ergs" that energize and guide behavior. (Yes, there were research theses and dissertations on "ergs.") By 1953, David McClelland was doing extensive work with Murray's "Thematic Apperception Test," which became a tool in research and clinical practice. McClelland first wrote about "needs," then later called them "expectations." The early version of the list included things like the needs for hunger, sex, aggression, fear, affiliation, power, achievement, deference, and on and on and on. The clinical and research literature on those "needs" is immense. They are all convenient fictions.

In the 1950s and 1960s, Abraham Maslow developed his immensely popular idea of "self-actualization." Scientists and the general public loved it, even though, by Maslow's definition, Adolph Hitler and Joseph Stalin were highly self-actualized persons. As part of his thinking about self-actualization, Maslow created an arbitrary "hierarchy of needs": physiological needs, safety needs, esteem needs, and the self-actualization need. Practically everyone loved Maslow's fictions, and scientists and clinicians created another huge body of literature. Today, much of that literature sits neglected on library shelves, just like the literatures for all of the fictitious needs that came before. In 1959, K. B. Madsen wrote about 12 "primary motives." You already know the rest of that story.

In 1965, William Glasser wrote *Reality Therapy*. In it, he described two "needs" that all people share. Later, he expanded his list of needs to five. In 1999, he seems to imply that there might be six needs; he calls "love and belonging" a single need, but he says that a person can be high on need for love and low on need for belonging, or the reverse. To me, it looks like he is describing two needs, not one, and that would make a total of six.

To see some recent examples of people who talk about needs, or similar alleged internal motivators, especially as those ideas are applied in schools, look at J. M. Jenkins, *Transforming High Schools: A Constructivist Agenda* (Technomic Publications, Lancaster, Pennsylvania, 1996). The discipline program in that book relies on "control theory," but it is Glasser's Control Theory, which he now calls Choice Theory. On page 111, you will see the following: "The behaviors that people choose are related to the satisfaction of one or more of the five basic needs. The behaviors they continue to choose are behaviors that in each person's mind reduces the disparity between what they want and what they have. The behaviors and their accompanying perceptions are specific and individual. In this context behavior actually controls perception (Glasser, 1981). Consequently, the key to controlling student behavior in school is to get them to behave differently so that their perception of school as a need-satisfying place changes." This source says that there are five needs. The author talks about "the key to controlling student behavior in school." Does that sound "just like RTP" or "exactly like PCT"?

Another recent source on the importance of needs in the classroom is V. F. Jones and L. S. Jones, *Comprehensive Classroom Management: Creating Positive Learning Environments for All Students*, fourth edition (Allyn & Bacon, Needham Heights, Massachusetts, 1995). It includes material about Rudolf Dreikurs, Stanley Coopersmith, William Glasser, David Elkind, and Joan Lipsitz. The authors also advance their own set of needs that children allegedly bring to the classroom. Of course, the numbers and names of the needs described by all of those people are different. Such is the nature of convenient fictions.

My visits to schools began in 1995. I have encountered several discipline programs whose creators argue that there are more, or fewer, needs than Glasser claims, and the names of the needs are not always the same. The multiplicity of numbers and names for alleged needs reflects the individual preferences of the authors, rather than something we all share because it is built into each of us by our common genetic heritage. *There is absolutely no scientific evidence to support William Glasser's claim that there are five (or is it six?) needs like the ones he proposes. His variable list of needs is a creation of his imagination.* Please do not misunderstand me. It is not necessarily a bad thing in itself if Glasser imagines that several needs are important in human behavior, but it is bad that many people believe the list is scientifically validated, and that, consequently, it should govern their actions in their private lives or in schools. People who want to act on their own beliefs that Glasser's list of needs is important should do that, but they should not tell anyone else that the "reality" of the needs on the list is "proven" by scientific research.

William Glasser's needs are abstract words. I doubt that any project designed to identify the entire set of genes in a species, like the human genome project or the *E. coli* genome project, will locate a single gene, or a set of genes, for anything like a "need for survival," much less for alleged needs like power, or freedom, or fun and belonging. This is one of several reasons that Glasser's "theory" cannot apply to all living things.

In PCT, we work with the idea of physiological "needs," or physiological requirements, that are generally recognized in biological science, like the required concentrations of certain nutrients and gases in the blood, or the required temperature at the core of the brain. We treat those required physiological levels as *reference perceptions*, specified in systems that control the magnitudes of perceptual signals related to actual physiological conditions. In other words, we construct our model of "physiological regulation" (which biologists call "homeostasis") as an example of perceptual control. We also construct our models of more "abstract" or "higher-level" perceptions, like "belonging" or "love," as examples of perceptual control, with people behaving to make the perceptions be the way they want them. The phenomenon of "survival" is probably something that simply happens as an unintended side effect, whenever an organism successfully controls all of the physiologically specified conditions. There is no convincing evidence that survival depends on an independent "need," or "instinct," or "drive."

Internal Motivation

Glasser: "Therefore, all behavior is internally motivated. This means that Choice Theory is diametrically opposed to the traditional, externally motivated, common sense psychology of the world, *Stimulus-Response (S-R) Theory. Since our motivation is completely intrinsic, the only behavior we can control is our own.*"

Bourbon: The idea that behavior is internally motivated runs as one of two uninterrupted and competing themes through the entire history of philosophy, from ancient to modern. The other theme asserts that the environment controls behavior.

The concept of internal motivation is central to nearly all cognitive theories, neurological theories, and neuro-cognitive theories. That concept, alone, is inadequate to explain behavior, for reasons I explained earlier. People do not control their *actions*. They control their *perceptions*. To do that, they allow their actions to vary, in any ways that are necessary, given the varying conditions of the world.

In all of his writings, William Glasser contrasts his ideas with "S-R theory." The issue is much bigger than that. All theories that explain behavior as the end product in a chain of causality are properly called *cause-effect* (*C-E*) theories. In all C-E theories, some antecedent cause, whether in the environment or inside the individual, causes behavior, as the end of the causal chain. No C-E theory can explain how a person controls perceptions by affecting events in the world. Only a properly designed circular-causal model, like the model in PCT, can explain the phenomenon of perceptual control.

I Believe That Glasser Either Misunderstood or Did Not Appreciate What Powers Taught Him

Glasser: "For many years, I used the term Control Theory for what I am now calling Choice Theory. Even though I had always believed that we are intrinsically motivated, I learned from an exponent, William Powers, a theoretician, that there is an actual theory of this motivation called Control Theory. In order for Control Theory to work for me as a practicing psychiatrist, psychotherapist and educator, I made many changes in what Powers taught me." Glasser's changes include the development of his five needs; the ideas of Total Behavior and The Quality World; deletion of Powers's idea that there are multiple levels of perception (replaced by Glasser with "the much more usable perceptual filters—the *Total Knowledge Filter* and the *Valuing Filter*"); and so on. "Finally, I replaced the concept of reorganization with creativity, because reorganization implies changing around what is already there. Creativity often means changing what is there to something totally new and more effective; for example, that the earth is round, not flat."

Bourbon: In this passage, I believe Glasser reveals that he did not understand when Powers explained control theory to him. What is more, I believe Glasser reveals his approach to building a "theory" of behavior as making changes that he likes aesthetically—he changed control theory to match his preferences for the way it sounded. Apparently, he did not care, or perhaps did not understand, that perceptual control theory is a formal theory that makes specific quantitative predictions about what will happen in certain circumstances. When we do our work the right way, those of us who recognize PCT as a scientific theory make changes only if they improve the predictive power of the theory, never simply because they make PCT sound nicer. Changes like those Glasser made render the theory useless for scientific work. I have no idea what Glasser means in his passage about how he improved on the idea of "reorganization," which is a process that we hypothesize in PCT to explain many kinds of learning.

I believe that Glasser misunderstood, or did not appreciate, what Powers taught him. I believe the evidence for this claim has been clear for many years. In May 1987, six years after he published *Stations of the Mind*, Glasser said in an interview published in *Phi Delta Kappan*: "In the course of my research, I came across a book, *Behavior: The Control of Perception*, written by William T. Powers and published by Aldine Press in 1973. I found the book obscure and difficult to understand, but Powers was one of the first to give the concepts of control theory (which, at that time, were engineering concepts) a biological application. Working a little bit with Powers and a great deal on my own, I refined those ideas and applied them to human behavior" (page 658).

I accept Glasser's remark that he personally found *BCP* difficult to understand; evidence to support that claim is abundant in his writings. However, Glasser's characterization of the subject of Powers's book is patently false. From his earliest papers in the 1950s, through *BCP* in 1973, to the present, there is no doubt whatsoever that Powers wrote about human behavior. The day in 1973 when I read Powers's article in *Science*, I knew immediately that he had invented an original psychology to explain the behavior and actions of all living things, which obviously includes people. Glasser's claim that Powers only applied control theory to biology, and that he, Glasser, applied it to humans, at the very least reflects Glasser's failure to understand what he read and heard from Powers.

Glasser Dissociates from PCT

For anyone who questions my belief that Glasser does not fully understand how people act to control their perceptions, or how scientific control theory differs from his personal speculations, I offer the following evidence.

Glasser: "Considering that I have always taught that we

choose all that we do, I decided in the spring of 1996 to call what I teach *Choice Theory*. I never liked the name, Control Theory, because it has implied external control. Also, since Powers and I teach so differently, I thought it misleading for me to continue to call what I teach Control Theory. Since I cannot remove the words Control Theory from all I have written, I ask you to read these words as Choice Theory. Everything else I have written that describes or explains this theory is still completely accurate. Changing the name makes it even more so."

Bourbon: Glasser repeats his claim that we choose "all that we do," which, by his definition, means we choose our behavior. He says that, in spite of the new name for his theory, everything he has ever written on the subject of how we choose our behavior is "still completely accurate." I think Glasser should have said that everything he wrote on that subject is still as accurate as it ever was. The scale of accuracy runs from "not at all" to "perfect."

I believe Glasser reveals a mistaken notion that perceptual control theory is like his Control Theory, in the sense that both are things that people can simply decide to teach, or not. For Glasser to renounce PCT is like an aerospace engineer saying that the physical laws of motion are just ideas that physicists teach, and she has decided to teach something different, something that she also uses when she designs airplanes. I would not want to fly in one of her planes.

Again, I think that Glasser's Reality Therapy is more humane and respectful of the client than many other psychiatric therapies. I believe that Glasser could have made RT even more effective, had he modified parts of it that are inconsistent with PCT. Glasser had many opportunities to make such changes, but instead he made wholesale changes to create his Control Theory, then finally changed the name and said that he renounced any association with PCT. One result of Glasser's actions has been decades of confusion, when people discovered his non-scientific CT and innocently believed it to be a scientific theory. Many people still think Glasser's Choice Theory is perceptual control theory. It is not.

Chronology of Powers's PCT,
Ford's Work, and Glasser's RT/CT

1950s–1960s

William T. Powers and two colleagues began to develop control systems theory, which was later renamed perceptual control theory.

Here is some information to help you decide on my suitability to write about the subjects in this chapter. I began my undergraduate studies in 1957 as a physics major who took a psychology course. Later I changed my major to history, then to psychology. In 1966, I finished my Ph.D. in physiological psychology and human perception. For at least a year after that, I occasionally had a dream in which I heard a knock on the door and awoke in the dream to see the committee of professors from my dissertation examination. They said that they had to take my degree back because "no one should have a degree for knowing that." I am no Freudian, but the meaning of the dream is clear: I thought my degree was not worth having. In spite of the dream, I spent the next seven years using and teaching ideas from "scientific" psychology that I thought were deeply flawed.

1965

William Glasser published *Reality Therapy* (Harper & Row, New York). In it, he said, "Psychiatry must be concerned with two basic psychological needs: the need to love and be loved and the need to feel that we are worthwhile to ourselves and to others" (pages 9–10).

1969

William Glasser published *Schools Without Failure*. The book contains the basic elements of what Glasser eventually called his "10 Steps to Good Discipline." He still said that there are two basic needs.

Ed Ford began to work with Glasser. Ford learned, taught, and applied many of the ideas described in Glasser's books; he was a therapist in RT and became a trainer for RT.

1973

Powers published a book, *Behavior: The Control of Perception*, and a *Science* article, "Feedback: Beyond Behaviorism." (Research and publications on PCT continue to the present, but I won't include any more citations of that work here.)

I read both of Powers's publications, and my life has not been the same since then.

1974

Glasser published an article, "New Look at Discipline," in *Learning: The Magazine for Creative Teaching*. In it, he further developed his "10 Steps."

1977

Glasser published an article, "10 Steps to Good Discipline," in *Today's Education: The Journal of the National Education Association*. In it, he further refined his "10 Steps."

Ed Ford and Steven Englund published *For the Love of Children: A Realistic Approach to Raising Your Child* (Anchor Press/Doubleday). In it, they acknowledged their debts to William Glasser. They relied heavily on techniques from Glasser's Reality Therapy. Scattered through the book are ideas similar to those in Glasser's "10 Steps." Ford and

Englund wrote about two basic needs, love and worth.

1980

I have heard that this was the year when someone gave Glasser a copy of Powers's *Behavior: The Control of Perception*, published seven years earlier. Before long, Glasser invited Powers to visit him to explain control theory. Earlier in this chapter, I discussed some of what ensued.

William Glasser's wife Naomi published an edited book, *What Are You Doing? Case Histories in Reality Therapy* (Harper & Row, New York), to which Ed Ford contributed two chapters.

1981

William Glasser published *Stations of the Mind*. (Powers wrote the Foreword.) In this book, Glasser began to add his own arbitrary and non-scientific revisions to control theory. Glasser is a medical doctor, but he tried to ground Reality Therapy and his version of control theory on ideas from pop neurology, as when he said that the five basic needs are located in the frontal lobes of the cerebral hemispheres. Even if we were to grant Glasser the existence of his five basic needs, claims like his about the frontal lobes are completely unverifiable.

Ed Ford was trained as a social worker. He is not a scientist, but in 1981 he began to suspect that there was more to control theory than Glasser said. Ed began to doubt that Glasser's interpretation of control theory was accurate, and he began to communicate with Powers. That was when I first heard of Ed.

1982

I organized the first meeting of people interested in Powers's control theory. Ed Ford was there. That gathering eventually led to the formation of the Control Systems

Group (CSG).

Ed Ford taught and used ideas found in Glasser's *Schools Without Failure*, but Glasser began to move away from, or modify, some of those ideas. Based on his major publications, it appears to me that Glasser had already abandoned his own "10 Steps to Good Discipline."

1984

Glasser published *Control Theory: A New Explanation of How We Control Our Lives* (originally titled *Take Effective Control of Your Life*). In it, he repeated his idea that everyone shares the same basic needs, determined by our genes (pages 5 and 9). He discussed four "psychological" needs: a need to belong, a need for power, a need for freedom, and a need for fun. After he gave his standard description of the needs, Glasser wrote the following: "It is not important to the thesis of this book that I establish with any certainty what the basic needs are that drive us. To gain effective control of our lives, we have to satisfy what we believe is basic to us and learn to respect and not frustrate others in fulfilling what is basic to them. All *you* will ever know is what drives you, just as I will know only what drives *me*. We cannot look into other people's heads and see what drives them. We can listen to what they tell us and look at what they do, but we should not make the mistake of assuming we *know* what drives them. This means that we can never be sure of satisfying anyone else no matter what we do. It is reasonably safe, however, to assume that what drives us is similar to what drives other people, so there is no harm in trying to satisfy another person. But if what we do does not work, we should not persist or we run the risk of losing that person for a friend or lover" (page 16).

To me, that paragraph is remarkable, in the light of all that Glasser wrote in the years that followed. In it, he came close to adopting a position like that in perceptual control theory: he acknowledged that no one can know with certainty what "drives" another person, and that when we satisfy ourselves, we should not frustrate others who are fulfilling themselves. So close! Of course, in PCT, we do not talk about something inside a person that "drives" his behavior. Glasser came close, but he immediately "bounced off" when he insisted that, even though we can never be sure of satisfying another person no matter what we do, we should go ahead and try, because they are probably like us anyway. If only he had stopped while he was ahead!

In the paragraph, Glasser seems to say that every person is driven by his or her own set of needs, which implies that the number of needs, and their names, can vary from person to person. In light of that claim, how could it be that, to the day in 1999 when I am writing this, Glasser and his followers still insist that we all share the same five genetically determined needs, and that those needs drive our behavior? To this day, when they talk about teachers in the classroom, Glasser, present associates, and many of his former associates say that teachers must meet all of the needs of all of their students, simultaneously. Does it sound "exactly like RTP" to say that "we can never be sure of satisfying anyone else no matter what we do," and then to go on and assign precisely *that* impossible task to all teachers, in all classrooms?

In this book, written in 1984, the "10 Steps" are gone. All that remains of them is a little material about how children must learn rules and about how to get them to make plans when they have broken the rules.

Glasser said, "The purpose of this book is to help increase our knowledge by attempting to teach the control theory through which we attempt to satisfy our needs" (page 18). That is a strange goal. Imagine that someone told you he wanted to teach you the gravitational theory through which you go to the refrigerator to take out the things you will eat for lunch. This is one of many times when Glasser has talked about a theory as something you *do* in your daily life, rather than as an organized attempt to *explain what you do*. He said you *do* something called Control Theory, rather than that control theory *explains what you do*. That confusion runs through all of Glasser's writings.

1986

Glasser published *Control Theory in the Classroom*. In it, his presentation of control theory continued to deteriorate. He emphasized the importance of the basic needs and said that "control theory explains that all of our behavior is always our best attempt at the time to satisfy at least five powerful forces which, because they are built into our genetic structure, are called basic needs" (page 14). I have given a critique of that idea above.

Glasser began to describe teachers as managers, in the sense of managers in business and industry. He said that, as managers, teachers are responsible for the happiness of every child in their classes. If the teacher has identified which needs are not met for each child, and if the teacher arranges the classroom so that all of those needs are met for all of the children, then the classroom will be perfect, and there will be no need for discipline. It is obvious that Glasser was moving to the idea that teachers are accountable for everything that happens in classrooms, an idea that ironically places Glasser in perfect agreement with all behavior-management programs that rely on theoretical ideas from operant conditioning and S-R theory.

1987

Ed Ford published the book *Love Guaranteed* (Harper & Row, San Francisco). In it, he demonstrated the results of his attempts to understand PCT and to incorporate principles from PCT in his counseling practice.

By this time, some differences between Ford and Glasser were very clear. Glasser continued to modify his non-scientific version of control theory to his own aesthetic ends; in contrast, Ford labored to better understand PCT and to modify his own practice accordingly. Ford continued to use many valuable clinical techniques he learned from

Glasser, but he understood that those techniques provided him a way to interact with people as living perceptual control systems, whose actions vary any way necessary to control their own perceptions. Glasser moved further into the idea that people are need-driven, and that they plan and select their behavior.

1989

Ed Ford published *Freedom from Stress* (Brandt Publishing). In it, he gave evidence of further developments in his understanding of PCT as it applied to his counseling practice. By this time, I was using Ford's two books about PCT and counseling in my experimental psychology classes at the university. I had students read one of the books at the start of the semester, as a "teaser." Ed's writing style is conversational and non-threatening. Most of my students, both graduate and undergraduate, "took the bait." They liked the practical techniques Ed described, and they got a small dose of PCT. During the remainder of the semester, I would always refer back to Ed's clinical examples while I led my students through the technical details of scientific PCT, including experiments and exercises in computer modeling. Years later, more of my former students remember and use ideas from Ed Ford's books than remember the technical details I worked so hard to get across to them!

1990

William Glasser published *The Quality School: Managing Students Without Coercion*. The title reveals that Glasser had moved even further from anything that resembles scientific control theory, toward the idea that teachers are managers, like those in business and industry. Glasser had discovered and become enthralled with the work on management by W. Edwards Deming. Even more than in his book *Control Theory in the Classroom*, Glasser laid the reponsibility squarely on teachers to identify and to meet the needs of all students in their classrooms. I will say more about his specific suggestions for discipline below.

1993

William Glasser published *The Quality School Teacher*. Scientifically, his presentation of control theory deteriorated even further. He said, "Control theory explains that we will work hard for those we care for (belonging), for those we respect and who respect us (power), for those with whom we laugh (fun), for those who allow us to think and act for ourselves (freedom), and for those who help us make our lives secure (survival)" (page 30). I see no reason at all why some of the relationships Glasser described in that passage should be labeled with the particular names he selected. From the perspective of PCT, the ideas in the passage are arbitrary assertions and do not represent what we know about people, viewed as living perceptual control systems.

Glasser said very little about discipline in this book. Problems are supposed to disappear from schools when teachers recognize and meet all needs for all students.

1994

Ed Ford started his Responsible Thinking Process (RTP) at Clarendon and Solano Schools in Phoenix. He tried to use principles from PCT to guide his development of RTP, and he used ideas from PCT to interpret its effects. It is clear that many features of RTP are similar to Glasser's earlier "10 Steps to Good Discipline." That is no surprise, given Ford's long association with Reality Therapy during the years when Glasser taught and used the "10 Steps." However, the distribution of responsibility and accountability in Ed Ford's process differs sharply from that in William Glasser's current program of Quality Schools and Choice Theory, and, viewed as a total program, RTP is not identical to Glasser's "10 Steps." Some of the questions are the same, but the total "packages" in which they are used, and the ways their roles are understood by their developers, are not at all alike. (I say more about that later.) What is more, by the early 1980s, Glasser had abandoned the "10 Steps," and in 1996, he renounced them altogether. In effect, Ed Ford revived an impressive discipline process that had been abandoned by Glasser, and he made it even more effective.

Ford published *Discipline for Home and School* (Brandt Publishing) to describe RTP and its effects at Clarendon School. Bill Powers wrote the Foreword. In the book, Ford described RTP as "Teaching children to respect the rights of others through responsible thinking based on perceptual control theory."

1995

News about RTP spread, and Ford began to teach people at schools in several states how to use it.

1996

In January, representing the scientific side of PCT, I traveled to Arizona to observe schools that used RTP. I looked specifically for evidence that RTP actually produced positive changes in schools, and that RTP had anything to do with PCT. I was satisfied on both counts. I obtained a grant to visit schools that use RTP and to study RTP's effectiveness. Under the grant, I also work with Ed Ford to improve the process and to introduce as much of PCT into RTP as is practicable.

Drawing on information gathered during visits to schools with me, Ford published the first edition of *Discipline for Home and School, Book Two* (Brandt Publishing). In this book, Ford described features of RTP that were found in every school where the process was working very well. He also described practices that led to RTP not working in some schools.

Using ideas from *Book Two* as his criteria, Ed Ford began

to certify schools that used RTP effectively. He also began to certify administrators and teachers directly responsible for RTP in successful schools.

William Glasser visited Australia and discovered that many people in schools there were not using his Quality School program the way he intended. In a flurry of letters, newsletters, and policy statements, he formally renounced all discipline programs, including his own "10 Steps to Good Discipline" that he had stopped using by the early 1980s. He renounced all associations between his own work and Powers's PCT, and he renamed his own theory Choice Theory. Glasser said that whenever you read something that he wrote earlier, you should read the words "Control Theory" as "Choice Theory." Glasser established a new institute, named after himself. He required that anyone who wanted to become a member must renounce all discipline programs and all ties to PCT. Earlier in this chapter, I described other changes that Glasser initiated in his program in 1996.

In the Winter 1996 issue of *The William Glasser Institute Newsletter*, Glasser announced that he was working on a new book, *Choice Theory: A New Psychology for a New Century*.

1997

More than 40 schools, in at least nine states, used RTP. During the summer, Ed Ford conducted workshops on RTP in Australia and presented information about RTP at conferences around the United States. He hosted his second annual workshop on RTP in Phoenix. Many people who attended the workshop also attended the annual meeting of the Control Systems Group in Durango, Colorado.

Ford published a greatly expanded second edition of his book, *Discipline for Home and School, Book One* (Brandt Publishing). It included numerous revisions, as well as several new chapters written by people who had used RTP successfully at their schools.

Several people who were associated with William Glasser for many years, including some whose work was individually rejected by him in 1996, declined his invitation to join the new William Glasser Institute. Instead, they formed the International Association for Applied Control Theory (IAACT). At the start, it was not clear how IAACT would define "control theory."

The Australian Reality Therapy Newsletter 9(1), 1997, included "A Message From Dr. William Glasser, To All Faculty, The Quality School Consortium Board and All Members of the Consortium." Here, Glasser repeated a now-frequent lament: "I deeply regret ever using my own reality therapy ideas to create the 'ten steps of discipline.' It was an honest mistake" (page 5). A few lines later, he said, "I have not taught or supported that program for over ten years, well before I created The Quality School" (page 5). The newsletter was published in 1997, and *The Quality School* was published in 1990. The most recent reference I can locate for a publication by Glasser specifically about his "10 Steps to Good Discipline" is from 1977. I conclude that he stopped advocating and developing the "10 Steps" at about the time that he encountered Powers's control theory. He has not published anything about the "10 Steps" for 20 years, at least not in any easily located source, and certainly not in any of his highly popular books. Anyone who thinks the program of "10 Steps" is still "Glasser's program" is mistaken; from Glasser's perspective in 1997, the "10 Steps" program is an unwelcome artifact from a distant past.

The April 1997 *Phi Delta Kappan* included "A New Look at School Failure and School Success" by William Glasser. In the article, Glasser described how difficult it was for people in schools to change from stimulus-response (S-R) practices to the practices he advocated for his Quality Schools. He wrote about how easy it was for people to cling to, or lapse back into, manipulative and punitive practices. On that topic, Glasser and Ford agree perfectly, although Ford now recognizes that the problem in many schools springs from traditional cause-effect practices, of which S-R practices are only a subset. (Nearly all so-called cognitive and neurological practices are also grounded in a cause-effect theory of behavior.) It is obvious that staff members who punish students create problems in many schools, and it is difficult for many of those people to give up their punitive techniques.

Glasser wrote that, in schools where people abandoned punitive manipulations and initiated positive, supportive interactions with students, learning improved and discipline problems declined. According to Glasser, students in those schools said that teachers cared about them. Again, I believe Ford would agree completely with that idea. When adults listen to children and politely ask them about what they are doing, the children often begin to believe that the adults care about them.

If Glasser's ideas, as reported in the *Phi Delta Kappan* article, and Ed Ford's ideas, as presented in his books, are close together on the issues I just described, then does that mean Ford's ideas are the same as Glasser's? No. The reason for my answer is simple. In the *Phi Delta Kappan* article, Glasser repeated the claim he has made for decades: "Choice theory teaches that we are all driven by four psychological needs that are embedded in our genes: the need to belong, the need for power, the need for freedom, and the need for fun" (page 599). Glasser clung firmly to his arbitrary needs. He also retained his idea that teachers must change the environment, specifically their own behavior, to meet students' needs: "In school, if he senses that Janet (the teacher) is now caring, listening, encouraging, and laughing, John (the student) will begin to consider putting her into his quality world" (page 600). It looks like Glasser is saying that the teacher must make the student sense her attitudes and emotions, so that perhaps the student "will begin to consider" changing himself. Ford recognizes the impossibility of such demands on teachers.

I do not claim that Glasser's program for quality schools is ineffective, or that it does not work. If the data Glasser reported in the *Phi Delta Kappan* are correct, then something positive happened in the two schools he described. I do contend that any positive changes that occurred were not caused when teachers met the needs that Glasser insists drive our behavior.

1998

Ford continued to teach his program at schools throughout the United States, in Australia, and in Singapore. He began work on a revised and expanded edition of *Discipline for Home and School, Book Two*.

The William Glasser Institute flourished. At its site on the World Wide Web, the Institute posted a description of Choice Theory that included Glasser's assertions "that all we do is behaving, that almost all behavior is chosen, and that we are driven by our genes to satisfy five basic needs." He stated that his CT "is offered to replace *external control theory*," his label for S-R theory. In a section of the web site titled "The Ten Axioms of Choice Theory," Glasser repeated some of the claims I just described and asserted that we have direct control over how we act and think. Does the material I have quoted from Glasser's web site seem to indicate that he has modified his personal beliefs in cause-effect to make them more compatible with PCT science? Are Glasser's assertions the same as PCT? You tell me.

Glasser published *Choice Theory: A New Psychology of Personal Freedom* (HarperCollins, New York). In it, he repeated the list of five basic needs and the "ten axioms" that I described from his web site (pages 332–336). He said, "The strength of each need is fixed at birth and does not change" (page 91). Glasser calls for extensive changes in curriculum and instructional practices and says that, when they are accomplished, there will be no discipline problems in schools. There will be occasional disciplinary incidents, but when they occur, teachers should use Reality Therapy to counsel students (pages 269). There were no fundamental changes in Glasser's program. He still said that teachers must create an environment that meets all of the students' alleged needs (those wonderfully convenient fictions). If a child disrupts, the teacher is responsible, and the teacher must do extra work to make things right. In Quality Schools, teachers do not expect children to change.

In this book, Glasser said some things about needs that seem at odds with what he said in earlier publications. For example, he said, "Even though we do not know what these needs are and may never know them to the extent I explain in this chapter, we start to struggle to satisfy them as soon as we draw our first breath" (page 28). He also said, "Most of us know nothing about our basic needs. What we know is how we feel . . ." (page 45). Those statements seem to contradict what Glasser wrote in 1984: "All *you* will ever know is what drives you, just as I will know only what drives *me*."

Once again, Glasser laments that he created the "10 Steps" that he abandoned long ago. He said, "For years, schools all over the country have been buying discipline programs that promise to get students in order in a coercive system. . . . I developed one myself in the 1970s, the Ten-Step Discipline Program based on reality therapy, and unfortunately it is still in use" (page 269).

In Chapter 5, "Compatibility, Personality, and the Strength of Needs," Glasser repeated some ideas from another recent book by him, *Staying Together*, where he said a person should select a mate by looking for a person with a "needs profile" like his or her own. Allegedly, the needs profile assesses the relative strengths of the five basic needs. One of the alleged needs is "need for love and belonging." However, Glasser said in *Choice Theory* that a person might be high in need for love, but low in need for belonging, or the reverse (page 104). To me, he seemed to say that these are really two different needs, which would mean that there are six basic needs, not five. From time to time, Glasser has changed the number of needs on his list, and their names, exactly the way other mainstream behavioral scientists change their lists.

Also in Chapter 5, Glasser asserted that a therapist can predict the needs profiles of people in various psychiatric diagnostic categories. Forget for a moment that the manual of psychiatric diagnostic categories changes every few years, often for reasons that are entirely political. Right now, I urge you to remember my earlier comments about the questionable history of "needs" in philosophy and psychology, and about the idea that needs are convenient fictions. The fictions created by people like Murray and Maslow were adopted more widely than those advocated by Glasser, and they were the objects of much more research than will ever be directed toward the needs on Glasser's list. Convenient fictions are not necessarily bad. In some situations, they can be very useful, but it is a serious mistake to believe that a particular set of needs has been "scientifically proved" to be real.

The IAACT met in Vancouver, British Columbia, Canada. Any doubts about how the IAACT would interpret control theory were resolved when the group unveiled a logo containing native Canadian symbols for each of "the five basic needs"—Glasser's five basic needs. The IAACT web site also declared "all behavior is purposeful and is intended to meet one of our five Basic Human Needs"; the familiar list followed. Members of the IAACT made the momentous decision to break away from Glasser's organization, but, as of this writing, they have not abandoned the convenient fiction of his five basic needs.

1999

It is late on an April evening in 1999. In a few minutes I will use e-mail to send the final revisions of this chapter to the editor. To check on the validity of my comparisons in this chapter, I just "visited" the web sites for the William Glasser Institute, the International Association for Applied Control Theory, and the Responsible Thinking Process. This is what I found at each web site.

At the site for the William Glasser Institute, under a section labeled "What We Stand For," there is a subsection titled "What Is Choice Theory." There, I found the following statement: "CHOICE THEORY is the basis for all programs taught by the Institute. It states that all we do is behave, that almost all behavior is chosen, and that we are driven by our genes to satisfy five basic needs: survival, love and belonging, power, freedom and fun."

At the site for the International Association for Applied Control Theory, I found the following statement on the first page: "Control Theory is the theory of human motivation and behavior based on the belief that we are internally motivated. That all behavior is purposeful and intended to meet one of our five Basic Human Needs; Belonging, Power, Freedom, Fun, & Survival."

At the site for the Responsible Thinking Process, I found the following statement on the first page: "Responsible Thinking Process (RTP)[:] A school discipline process that trains educators how to teach students to take responsibility for themselves by learning to think on their own, to respect the rights of others, to make effective plans, and to build self-confidence. The process is based on perceptual control theory (PCT)."

Do the program-defining statements on those three web sites look "exactly the same?" You tell me.

Summary of My Conclusions Based on the Chronology

There is no doubt whatsoever that William Glasser's work in schools reflects an understanding of what people are, and how they function, that is different from the understanding in Ed Ford's Responsible Thinking Process. On the one hand, Glasser says that people select and control their behavior so as to satisfy a number of genetically programmed needs. He also says that teachers are responsible for meeting the needs of all children in their classrooms; if the teachers do that, then there will be no problems and no need for discipline. Glasser never tried to modify his practices to match the principles of perceptual control theory; instead, he tried to change control theory to match his practices. Recently, Glasser renounced all ties with perceptual control theory.

On the other hand, Ed Ford has become increasingly involved in the Control Systems Group, comprising people who study and develop perceptual control theory. Even though he is not a scientist, Ford has worked to understand the formal theory and the behavioral model from PCT. (I know about his efforts firsthand from the many hours he spent talking to me on the phone, and into the early morning hours at CSG meetings.) Each time Ed thought that his understanding had improved, he wrote another book about the implications and applications of PCT in counseling and daily life. He adapted his practices to changes in his understanding of PCT, rather than the other way around. All the while, he continued to use many procedures he had learned as a member of Glasser's organization, including some questions and strategies from Reality Therapy, and elements of the "10 Steps to Good Discipline." However, he continuously modified his use of those techniques to bring them in line with his growing knowledge of PCT.

For example, Ed Ford recognizes that people always act to control how they perceive some parts of the world, and that to do so, their actions must vary to counteract inevitable disturbances that come from the world. When people share an environment, sooner or later, one of them will disturb someone else, either accidentally or deliberately. When that happens, a conflict might ensue. Ed's program tries to help children, and adults, learn how to control their own perceptions without unduly disturbing one another, and to help them learn how to resolve any conflicts that occur, when they inevitably do disturb one another.

The differences between Ford's and Glasser's understandings of people are reflected, directly, in what happens in schools that use their ideas, a topic I discuss next.

A Comparison of Certain Features from Ed Ford's Responsible Thinking Process and William Glasser's Quality Schools and Choice Theory

Why Do People Behave?

I have described differences between the explanations of human behavior promoted by William Glasser and those of perceptual control theorists. Those two explanations lead to profoundly different implications for what happens in classrooms. The differences are so great that they offer a classic example of just how important it is for us to examine the theories behind our practices.

Contemporary social scientists often dismiss theories as mere guesses, or as arbitrary declarations of personal bias. That is not true of scientific theories. Far from being a mere guess or a biased statement, a scientific theory is a summary of what we think we know about a subject—a summary expressed in a way that allows us to experimentally test the legitimacy of our ideas. Perceptual control theory is that kind of testable scientific theory. William Glasser's ideas are not. I do not say that in a derogatory sense. It is simply a fact that Glasser's "theories" can be characterized as guesses, or as declarations of personal preference, but not as testable scientific theories.

In his newsletters, Glasser has said that his basic program for schools is the one first described in *The Quality School*, so we must look there to see what Glasser believes should be happening in schools. Remember that Glasser says every time you read the words "control theory," you should replace them with "Choice Theory."

To understand what motivation actually is, it is necessary first to understand that control theory contends that all human beings are born with five basic needs built into their genetic structure: survival, love, power, fun, and freedom. All of our lives we must attempt to live in a way that will best satisfy one or more of those needs. Control theory is a descriptive term because we try to control our own behavior so that what we choose to do is the most need-satisfying thing we can do at the time. (pages 43–44)

Our genes, which in essence are the biological instructions for what we are to become, not only dictate what our structure is to be (for example, our eye color) but also (and this claim is unique to control theory) how we, as humans, must attempt to live our lives. Just as a northern migrating bird must always attempt to fly south for the winter, we, too, must attempt to live our lives in ways that we believe will best satisfy our needs. If what we are asked to do in school does not satisfy one or more of these needs or we do not care for the teacher who asks us to do it, then we will do it poorly or even not at all.

From birth, our behavior is always our best attempt at the time to do what we believe will best satisfy one or more of our needs. We can no more deny that these needs exist and are constantly on our mind (whether we are aware of it or not), than we can deny the shape of our nose or the color of our eyes. And regardless of our cultural background, we are all members of the same species, and all of us have the same genetic needs. We spend our lives trying to learn how to satisfy these needs, but most of us do not have a clear idea of what they are, especially when we are young. What we always know, however, is how we feel. And what we actually struggle for all of our lives is to feel good. It is from our ability to feel, essentially from our ability to know whether we feel good or bad, that most of us gain some idea of what our needs are. (page 44)

Glasser goes on to explain that students become disenchanted with school when it does not feel as good anymore. When they question why, they are told to work hard, and the rewards will come later. But, unfortunately, "the genetic needs themselves know nothing about later: They are continually pushing us to do what feels good now" (page 46).

In a nutshell, Glasser's theory says that everyone behaves to satisfy the same five basic needs, that those needs are coded in our genes, and that the needs operate in a cause-effect manner to drive our behavior or our actions. He also says that, when our behavior is right, our needs are met, and that in schools, problems occur when adults fail to meet all of the students' needs. If you are drawn to Glasser's ideas about needs, I urge you to review my analyses of the "needs" concept. Perceptual control theorists believe that not even our genes act as linear cause-effect devices, the way Glasser describes them. In PCT, we work with the idea that genes are parts of biochemical control systems, and that they do not "dictate" anything.

Perceptual control theory explains our actions as the means by which we control our perceptions. In PCT, there are no prior assumptions about which perceptions a person controls at any given time, or about why the person controls those particular perceptions at that particular time. We recognize that most controlled perceptions are not universal; some are highly idiosyncratic. To control a perception, a person must act to eliminate or prevent the effects of environmental disturbances that would otherwise make the perception change from what the person wants it to be. The person must behave in a way that cancels out the effects of the disturbances, or "opposes" the effects of the disturbances. That kind of opposition is not "good or bad" morally. A man is not necessarily good or bad when his actions cancel the effects of influences that would make his automobile veer from the path he intends. A woman is not necessarily good or bad when her actions cancel the effects of influences that would cause her lecture to deviate from the topics she intends. Instead, opposition to disturbances is the necessary means by which a person controls a perception. Unavoidably, every one of our actions produces many consequences in the environment, not just the consequences that oppose disturbances to our own perceptions. The additional consequences are unintended by us, and we are usually unaware of them. We don't realize that we just cut in front of another driver, we don't know that we are leaving a thermal image of our backside on the chair, we don't realize that our words uttered to one person were overheard by someone else who took offense.

No person can control another person's perceptions, nor can one person make another decide to control any particular perception. When people are close together in physical space and each behaves to control his or her own perceptions, it is inevitable that, sooner or later, one person will disturb another's controlled perceptions. One way we can disturb another person is unintentionally, by way of unintended consequences of our own actions. Of course, it is also possible for one person to disturb another deliberately. In a school, disturbances are often called "disruptions." It is inevitable that disturbances and disruptions will occur from time to time, sometimes unintentionally, sometimes on purpose. You tell me whether Ford and Powers are saying the same thing as Glasser on the subject of why people behave.

In the Classroom, Who Is Responsible for What?

Both William Glasser and Ed Ford believe that teachers have a right to teach to the best of their abilities, and students who want to learn have a right to learn in safety. That said, Glasser and Ford differ markedly on the subject of who is responsible for what, in the classroom.

Glasser's ideas about responsibility are very clear. Teachers must arrange the environment in the school in general, and in the classroom in particular, so that the environment meets all of the needs of all of the students simultaneously. If they do that, then discipline problems will disappear. If there are any residual discipline problems in a school, then the teachers have failed to satisfy all of the needs of all of the students. Quoting again from *The Quality School*: "Like boss-managers, lead-managers have the goal of getting their workers to work hard, but to do this, they continually keep the needs of the workers in mind" (page 42). Glasser says that teachers have to work to become part of the students' quality world. Even though he said earlier that people are all intrinsically motivated, he states that "students will not work hard for a teacher who is not firmly embedded in their quality worlds. A teacher must expend more time and effort trying to satisfy a student than an industrial manager needs to do for a worker" (page 66).

All through *The Quality School*, Glasser repeats the message that teachers must work hard to create conditions that encourage and persuade students to perform well. There is no doubt that he envisions teachers as managers of student behavior. Neither is there any doubt that, if students do not perform well, the responsibility rests on the teachers. That idea leads to his often-repeated claim that we must change the system, not the children. On the one hand, William Glasser says that everyone is internally motivated, but on the other hand, he says that students do not learn unless the outside world is "just right," and someone other than the students is responsible for making it "just right." The teacher is responsible for making the environment in the classroom "just right." Teachers are to accomplish that task by satisfying the needs that Glasser says all students share. He says repeatedly that when adults make the school satisfy the needs of all students simultaneously, disruptions vanish and there is no need for discipline.

A clear example of how Glasser's needs-driven theory turns into a specific procedure in the classroom is described on page 48 of *The Quality School*: "Learning together as a member of a small learning team is much more need-satisfying, especially to the needs for power and belonging, than learning individually." In that simple remark, I believe Glasser reveals a willingness to impose an arbitrary system of needs on everyone, and to trivialize the differences among people that might result in some students preferring to work alone. The preferences of those "loners"

Practical Standards for Schools

would be willfully trampled if a teacher were to follow
Glasser's arbitrary system for categorizing behavior according to five basic needs. Perceptual control theorists know
that such a flagrant disregard for the interests of individual
students would constitute massive disturbances for many
of them. Those disturbed students would be highly likely
to act to cancel the effects of the disturbances; they might
very well disrupt the "cooperative-learning classroom"
where they were not allowed to study alone.

Ed Ford realizes that teachers could never meet all of the
needs of all students, even if there really were five basic
needs. What teachers can do is try to help students learn
how to control their own perceptions without needlessly
disturbing others. When disturbances occur, either intentionally or unavoidably, teachers can try to help students
learn how to resolve the conflicts that are likely to ensue.
In the Responsible Thinking Process, teachers are responsible for teaching to the best of their ability and for following the RTP process. Students are responsible for learning
the content of the course, for minimizing avoidable disturbances to others, and for learning how to resolve the
results of disturbances that they cannot avoid. Ford's RTP
sounds very simple. It is. You tell me whether RTP is identical to Glasser's programs, with regard to who is responsible for what, in the classroom.

What Should Teachers Do When Students Disrupt?

According to William Glasser, once a school becomes a
Quality School, the needs of all students are met and there
are no discipline problems. In spite of that frequent asser-
tion, Glasser acknowledges that sometimes discipline problems still occur. In *The Quality School*, and in recent
newsletters, he has said that alternative discipline procedures will be necessary for a few years before a school
becomes a Quality School. In the book, he described several different procedures to use with students, for disruptions of various degrees of severity. "In the quality school

program we should not use any discipline program, even if it is seen as being based on Choice Theory and Reality Therapy, such as the ten steps of discipline and restitution. Also, we should not use any other program labeled or perceived as a discipline program." How much Glasser's ideas have changed over the years since he wrote *The Quality School* is apparent when he tells his associates that "we must be strong enough to resist demands for help with discipline and for discipline programs and offer them lead-management practices that will both eliminate the problems and deal with any problem, no matter how severe, that occurs in any school whether it is just beginning or far along the way toward becoming a Quality School."

"To answer the second question, what to do with a highly disruptive student: learn who they are and reach out to them when they are not disrupting." The teacher should use various strategies to engage disruptive students, and should play the role of a "social director" for them. "Finally, if all of this doesn't work, there is only one thing to do when a student is so disruptive that a teacher cannot teach, or students cannot learn. This is not counseling, it is quick and non-punitive. If you think you can keep the student in the room, get a comfortable chair, like an old easy chair, and immediately when the child disrupts, tell him to go take a rest. It is very important that all you say is: 'Take a rest.' Go to him when he settles down and evaluate if he needs reality therapy counseling, but try not to counsel him at the time. Try to integrate him back into the class and offer counseling later. If he does not settle down in the chair he must be removed from the room to a time-out room as described in several places in *The Quality School*. Remember, do this and only this so all children know you do not play games." (All quotations above are from "A Message from Dr. William Glasser," dated May 22, 1996, and reproduced in *Australian Reality Therapy News* 9(1) 1997.)

In *The Quality School*, Glasser wrote that a student should stay in the time-out room long enough to satisfy the classroom teacher, and long enough to work out an (unspecified) plan to stay out of trouble in the future. He encouraged classroom teachers to "reward" students who make a plan, for "trying." Also in the book, but not in recent newsletters, Glasser said that any student whose disruptions endanger teachers or other students should be sent home for three days, and the sentence should be renewed as long as the student is unwilling to return to school peacefully. It is difficult to think of a procedure that is any more in the tradition of cause-effect, or stimulus-response, than that one: if you "do time" (serve a sentence) on suspension from school, it will make you behave.

Ed Ford's RTP relies on a series of questions that the teacher asks whenever a student disrupts in a classroom or in any other locale in a school. The questions are like those in the "10 Steps to Good Discipline" that Glasser has repudiated. Ford uses the questions to help students focus their attention on what they are doing, on how their actions are related to the rules that apply in their present setting, and on how they might achieve their own goals (control their own perceptions) without running afoul of the rules in the future. Ford thinks of the rules as guidelines that help students and adults know the limits within which they can act to control their own perceptions, without needlessly disturbing other people. The rules also provide guidelines for how to resolve conflicts that occur when one person disturbs another.

A student who continues to disrupt goes to the responsible thinking classroom (RTC) to think about what has happened and to learn to prepare a specific plan for how to return to the classroom and avoid similar problems in the future. The student negotiates the plan with the classroom teacher. When the plan is acceptable to both parties, the student returns to class. RTP is designed to help students learn to manage their own affairs, controlling their own perceptions without needlessly disturbing other people. In Ford's program, teachers are not responsible for meeting a set of presumed universal needs, shared by all students. Instead, teachers simply teach their subjects and use the process consistently.

In difficult cases, where a student leaves the regular classroom many times and goes to the RTC, the professional staff work to discover which perceptions the student is controlling by going to the RTC. Ford recommends a special intervention team to examine each such case. The team comprises the RTC teacher, the classroom teacher, the parents, perhaps the school counselor or psychologist, and any other people with useful information about the child, or with access to resources that might help the child. In nearly every case where a child makes frequent visits to the RTC, educators discover that the student is experiencing difficult conditions at home or elsewhere, and they develop a special plan to help the student learn how to deal with those circumstances without disturbing other people. For example, in one school, the intervention team studied the situation of a young man who alternated between long periods when he never went to the RTC, and brief periods when he disrupted and went to the RTC very often. The team discovered that, during the times when he went often to the RTC, the young man was being sold by his older brother as a sexual "boy toy" for wealthy men. The school could not make that boy's situation different when he was away from the campus, but they devised a plan that helped him succeed while he was at school. The key to a successful discipline program is as profound and simple as that. You tell me whether Ford and Glasser say identical things about what teachers should do when a student disrupts.

Conclusion

I hope this chapter has helped you to better understand the relationships among Ed Ford's Responsible Thinking Process, William Powers's perceptual control theory, and the ideas of William Glasser. As I have said before, I hold Glasser's Reality Therapy in high regard as one of several effective present-centered therapies. However, I do not have the same high opinion of the scientific merit of

Glasser's "theories," or of the way he portrays his role in the development of control theory. Nor do I think highly of the way Glasser's program, with its needs-driven theory of behavior, requires teachers to explain all behavior as driven by five or six arbitrary needs that teachers must satisfy for all students. In contrast to my assessment of Glasser's theoretical utterances, I respect Ed Ford's attempts to incorporate PCT into RTP. When Ford designed RTP, he attempted to acknowledge the fact that both teachers and students always behave to control their own perceptions. Does that mean that RTP follows, necessarily, from PCT, or that RTP is the only possible process that could incorporate principles from PCT? The answer to both questions is no.

Ed Ford's RTP incorporates principles from PCT; there is no reason to assume that it is the only possible process that could do so. For example, I can imagine a process that more directly incorporated the "method of levels" (MOL), a technique William Powers developed as a way to study the hierarchical organization of human perception. The MOL is used by a few counselors and therapists. In certain ways, Ford's RTP achieves effects similar to MOL, especially when a student answering the RTP questions begins to think about the context of his or her actions, and about the consequences that he or she causes for other people. Nonetheless, Ed Ford's RTP is not identical to MOL, and neither RTP nor MOL is perceptual control theory.

I can also imagine a process in which someone combined features of William Glasser's program for Quality Schools, like the practices he suggests for developing curricula and for grading, with features of Ed Ford's RTP. Such a process could be consistent with principles from PCT. Of course, its creator would probably abandon Glasser's idea that behavior is driven by a specific set of needs, replacing it with the ideas that all people behave to control their perceptions and that the perceptions some people control are highly idiosyncratic. Probably many different processes could be designed that would be consistent with the principles of PCT science.

Here, I have not discussed any discipline programs other than Ford's and Glasser's, even though there are many other programs. Some people tout their programs as applications of operant conditioning theory, while others say that their programs incorporate the principles of cognitive science and neurological science, and still others assert that their programs embrace principles from both conditioning theory and cognitive science. My analyses of some of these programs reveal that many of them share the same model for how events happen in the world. Virtually all discipline programs rely on theories that say cause-effect operates in a direct, linear fashion. You tell me whether discipline programs like that are identical to Ed Ford's RTP.

Appendix 1
Responsible Thinking Process Card

To receive three copies of the 3" by 5" card reproduced here, send a stamped self-addressed envelope to RTP, Inc., 10209 N. 56th St., Scottsdale, AZ 85253.

RESPONSIBLE THINKING PROCESS (RTP)

A discipline program that creates mutual respect
by Edward E. Ford - based on perceptual control theory
from his books - **Discipline for Home and School, Books 1 & 2**

For children to succeed, they must believe you care about them, that you have confidence in their ability to solve problems, and they must experience mutual respect. The stronger the relationship, the easier it is to resolve differences. If done in a calm, respectful environment, this responsible thinking process can help build the relationship. It also teaches self-discipline through responsible thinking. Ask questions in a calm, respectful, curious voice. Never yell or tell, always ask. Avoid excuses by not asking why.

- **WHAT ARE YOU DOING?**

WHAT ARE THE RULES? or **IS THAT O.K.?**

WHAT HAPPENS WHEN YOU BREAK THE RULES?

IS THIS WHAT YOU WANT TO HAPPEN?

WHERE DO YOU WANT TO BE? or
WHAT DO YOU WANT TO DO NOW?

- **WHAT WILL HAPPEN IF YOU DISRUPT AGAIN?**

WHEN CHILDREN AVOID DEALING WITH YOU

If they avoid answering a question, repeat it. If they persist in not dealing with you, then ask . . .

DO YOU WANT TO WORK AT THIS OR NOT?

If they continue to avoid dealing with you, or, if after settling down, they again begin to disrupt, it means they don't want to follow the rules and have chosen to go to a restricted area. Then you say . . .

I SEE YOU HAVE CHOSEN TO LEAVE.

Once you have said this, never back down. The child must leave at once and go to a restricted area. Once they decide they want to return and obey the rules, they must be taught how to create a detailed plan, and how to use this plan to negotiate with the person in charge of where they were disrupting.

TEACH CHILDREN HOW TO CREATE AN EFFECTIVE PLAN

This process helps them organize their thinking and teaches them how to create successful plans. It builds the self-discipline and self-confidence necessary to successfully resolve future conflicts.
1. Work on one specific problem at a time.
2. Set a measurable goal so they know how they are doing.
3. Help them think through then explain a precise, detailed action plan on how they're going to achieve their measurable goal.
4. Create a chart or monitor form as an aid to achieving their goal.
5. Find someone to whom they can report their progress.

(continued on back)

These questions may help when creating a plan:

HOW ARE YOU GOING TO DEAL WITH THIS PROBLEM THE NEXT TIME IT HAPPENS?

WHAT WILL WE SEE HAPPEN IF YOU SUCCEED?

CREATE MUTUAL RESPECT WHILE NEGOTIATING PLANS

Negotiating is a critical part of the process. During negotiations, you should always use questions when dealing with a student. This teaches the child to think. When children approach a teacher, parent, or supervisor to negotiate their way back to where they were disrupting, they should be given time to explain how they were going to deal with their problem the next time it happens. Normally, this interchange shouldn't take more than 3 to 5 minutes. If part of their plan is unacceptable, various alternatives should be offered. Their plan should never be ignored or refused. If done properly, this process should improve the relationship between the child and the adult.

QUALITY TIME: THE KEY TO A STRONG RELATIONSHIP

LOVE - Willingness to spend quality time every day alone with another no matter how your partner behaves and without trying to control the other person.

CRITERIA FOR QUALITY TIME

1. DO ACTIVITIES THAT PROMOTE AWARENESS OF EACH OTHER AND CREATE PLEASURE THROUGH MUTUAL EFFORT.

such as:	not:
playing games	watching TV or movie
exercising together	just being together
working in a business or at home	taking a drive
doing projects or hobbies	listening to music
taking a walk or a bike ride	watching others

2. DO QUALITY TIME ACTIVITIES ALONE TOGETHER, NOT WITH OTHERS.
3. DO YOUR ACTIVITIES ON A REGULAR BASIS.
   A minimum goal should be at least 30 to 40 minutes per day, five to six days a week. With children, at least 20 minutes per day.

To guarantee a close intimacy, both must be totally committed to spending quality time alone together on a regular basis.

QUALITY TIME ILLUSIONS - Eating together, talking together, and physical intimacy - these activities do not create strong relationships, they can only enhance a committed love that already exists.

RTP, Inc. • 10209 N. 56th St. • Scottsdale, Arizona 85253
Phone: 480-991-4860

Appendix 2
Newspaper Reports on RTP

The following article, written by Hal Mattern, appeared in *The Arizona Republic* (Phoenix) on November 20, 1994. It is reprinted here with permission. Copyright © 1994 by *The Arizona Republic*.

Discipline Transforms School

New Expectations Improve Kids' Conduct

Although her job is to teach sixth-graders at Clarendon Elementary School, Pauline Rudloff used to spend nearly as much time scolding as educating.

Quarrels, fights and other disruptions were so common that Clarendon teachers ranked discipline as the No. 1 concern at the central Phoenix school last year.

"It was hard work to keep the students in line," said Rudloff, who has taught for 25 years. "I would have to take time out from the class to solve the problems."

But things are different this year at the school, at 12th and Clarendon avenues.

Since a schoolwide discipline program was installed earlier this year, disruptions have declined dramatically, and the teachers have found themselves with more time to do what they were hired to do.

"Now, I spend more time teaching than trying to be a counselor," Rudloff said. "This program has been a real help. It has taken a great burden off my shoulders."

The program, "Teaching Responsible Thinking" was developed by Edward E. Ford, a Phoenix social worker, counselor and author of *Discipline for Home and School*.

It is based on the theory that once children learn to think responsibly, their behavior automatically will change to conform to the rules or standards of wherever they are— the classroom, the cafeteria, the playground or even the school bus.

"The only way to teach children to act responsibly is to ask them to search their own minds and think for themselves," said Ford, whose program also is being used in schools in five other states.

"You can't try to control what they do. You can only teach them to control themselves."

That is accomplished by giving the students a choice, whether they want to straighten up and remain in class or leave until they decide to behave acceptably.

If they choose to continue their disruptive ways, the students are sent to the school's Pupil Responsibility Center, which is staffed by a teacher and an aide. The center is similar to the "time out" or detention rooms used at schools across the nation.

At other schools, however, students are sent back to class after serving their allotted time in detention with no real incentive to shape up. At Clarendon, they cannot return to class until they develop a plan outlining how they will change their behavior.

The students then have to take the plan to the teacher who threw them out of class and negotiate their return.

"They have to go back to the person and resolve the problem and convince them that they will change," said LeEdna Custer, the school's psychologist.

"If the teacher agrees, they can come back in. If they are not serious about changing, they go back to the PRC. It teaches them to take responsibility for their actions."

There are no threats of punishment involved in the program, nor do teachers yell at students, argue with them or order them to stop what they are doing. If students disrupt a class, the teacher asks a series of questions: What are you doing? What are the rules? What happens when you break the rules? Is that what you want to happen? What would you rather be doing? What do you want now?

The questions force the students to think about their behavior and to decide whether they would rather stay in class or go to the center.

"We're saying that it's OK to be there, but you have to respect the rights of the other kids to learn and of the teacher to teach," Ford said. "You have to respect the rules."

When the program was first started at Clarendon in February, the Pupil Responsibility Center was packed with misbehaving students. However, once those pupils realized what they would have to do to get back into class, the numbers declined quickly.

"They know that we are serious, and that we are going to follow through," said Del Merrill, principal at Clarendon.

"After they cycle through the PRC a few times, the majority of them back off."

In fact, teachers say that all they have to do in most cases is ask the first question: What are you doing?

"The minute you start to ask the question, it lets them know they have to shape up," said Christine Dilworth, a fifth-grade teacher.

"It usually takes only a few seconds to solve the problem."

The program also has prompted students to negotiate problems amongst themselves. When fights do start, onlookers now are more likely to stop them than to encourage them.

Another indication that the program is affecting students can be found on the wall of the center, where Darleen Martin, a teacher and counselor who runs the room, has posted letters from students who went through the program last spring.

"Thank you for listening to my problems and understanding them," one of the students wrote.

Serious cases of misbehavior still occur occasionally at Clarendon, which serves 600 fourth-, fifth- and sixth-graders.

Despite their young ages, some of the school's students

are involved in gangs, and many of them lack adequate social skills to deal with each other. In the past, that has resulted in constant conflict and the challenging of teachers by students.

"Everybody feels safer this year," Martin said. "Last year, there were some sixth-graders who were always intimidating people. We aren't letting that happen now. We are nipping it in the bud."

The discipline program at Clarendon was instigated by parents, teachers and school administrators. The school's parent-teacher association funded a series of weekend seminars by Ford, and several teachers and school-staff members attended on their own time.

The program is now used consistently by everyone at the school, including teachers, administrators, cafeteria workers, office clerks, janitors and bus drivers. Some parents even use the system at home.

"I have five children, and this is the first time I've felt I knew how to handle them effectively," said Sally Bruso, a Clarendon parent who attended Ford's seminars.

Ford's program also is being used at schools in New York, Michigan, Iowa, Idaho and Texas, and he has employed it at correctional and mental-health facilities.

Three other schools in the Osborn School District— Solano and Encanto elementary schools and Osborn Middle School—also have implemented the program, based largely on Clarendon's success.

Now that discipline is no longer the main concern at Clarendon, school officials have begun concentrating on teaching strategies and ways to help kids learn, assistant principal George Venetis said.

"Isn't that what it's all about?" he asked.

Statistics Show Success [sidebar]: Disturbances at Clarendon Elementary School have decreased since the implementation of a schoolwide discipline program last spring. Here are comparative statistics for the months of September and October in 1993 and 1994.

204   *Practical Standards for Schools*

Disturbance	'93	'94
Physical assaults	28	7
Fights	27	7
Weapons possession	6	0
Truancies	11	7

The following editorial appeared in *The Phoenix Gazette* on November 22, 1994. It is reprinted here with permission. Copyright © 1994 by *The Phoenix Gazette*.

Three 'Rs of Behavior

Often, too often, educators are the lightning rod of criticism for what's wrong with public schools, rather than being hailed for their accomplishments in classrooms of clashing behavioral standards.

Edward Ford is one who should be applauded. He found the key to diffusing classroom conflicts while detonating a child's desire to learn.

As a Phoenix social worker and counselor, Mr. Ford saw the demoralizing effect of students who sabotaged the educational process with their disruptions. He didn't think teachers should have to play cop and counselor while precious teaching time eroded away.

But most importantly, Mr. Ford did something about it. He created a lesson plan for teachers that reduces disciplinary problems because it teaches students how to be responsible for their own actions.

What Mr. Ford developed isn't a time- or money-consuming social program. Instead, it's a plan called Teaching Responsible Thinking. Mr. Ford believes, and has proven, that once students learn to think responsibly, their behavior will follow.

The program is amazingly simple. Perhaps even a generation or so ago, it wouldn't have been hailed as a novel concept. But today's students, and their parents, are different. Many lack the social skills to differentiate between abnormal and socially acceptable behavior. They haven't mastered taking responsibility for their actions, or changing their behavior.

At Clarendon Elementary in the Osborn Elementary School District, students are learning the three 'Rs of behavior: rules, respect and responsibility. And in less than a year, school officials saw physical assaults, fights, weapon possession and truancies dramatically drop while academic performance improved.

While the concept seems simple, execution is a bit more challenging.

A classroom infraction triggers a line of specific and sequenced questions. What are you doing? What are the rules? What happens when you break the rules? Is that what you want to happen? What do you want to do now?

It doesn't take long for most students to pick up on the conversational cues that their behavior is inappropriate, and it comes with consequences.

For those who don't catch on, they're excused from the classroom. These students go to a special center where they are isolated with other problem students. Knowing that most students would rather be with their friends than secluded with mischief-makers, motivation is added for them to follow the rules.

However, the beauty of Mr. Ford's program is that before problem students can return, they must make amends with their classroom teacher and show that their behavior has changed. This reinforces the message that education is a privilege that must not be taken for granted.

Mr. Ford's program works because he took a page or two from the old school, but with a modern twist. Students know what is expected and what won't be tolerated as behavioral standards are consistently applied. The twist is that students are empowered to learn self discipline and initiative in the process.

Appendix 3
Presentation to the American Educational Research Association

In the fall of 1993, I was asked by the administrators of Clarendon Elementary School in Phoenix, Arizona, to use their school as a model for a discipline program I had developed based on perceptual control theory. Clarendon School consists of seven fourth, fifth, and sixth grades and is in a multi-cultural, inner-city area. Once the staff had given a strong commitment and received adequate training, the program was initiated on January 24, 1994.

The basic principle of PCT is to understand and treat children as self-regulating systems whose behavior is their means of trying to control what matters to them. Self-direction and responsibility are developed by asking them specific questions which request them to review the consequences of what they've done and whether they want to respect the rights of others and remain where they are or to leave. If they choose to leave, they are sent to the social skills classroom. They remain there until they choose to return. If they are disruptive in the social skills classroom, they are taken home.

When they ask to return, they are first taught by the social skills teacher how to make a specific plan and then how to use their plan to negotiate with the person in charge of the place from which they came.

This program is explained further in my book, *Discipline for Home and School*, published by Brandt Publishing. For more information on this program or to obtain a book, write RTP, Inc., 10209 N. 56th St., Scottsdale, Arizona 85253. Phone 480-991-4860. The following statistics reflect the success of this program:

Table 1. Acts Deemed "Serious Acts of Misconduct"

	8/93–3/94	8/94–3/95	% Decrease
Physical Assaults	98	37	62
Weapons	16	0	100
Fighting	85	34	60
Theft	30	22	27

Table 2. Demographics

Current			At Implementation		
Ethnic Breakdown 1994–95 February 1995			Ethnic Breakdown 1993–94 January 1994		
Ethnic Group	Clarendon		Ethnic Group	Clarendon	
	#	%		#	%
Caucasian/ White	288	47.52	Caucasian/ White	283	52.21
Pacific Islander/ Asian	31	5.11	Pacific Islander/ Asian	22	3.87
Hispanic	180	29.70	Hispanic	145	26.76
African American	39	6.45	African American	40	7.38
Native American	68	11.22	Native American	53	9.77
TOTAL	606		TOTAL	542	

Percentage of students currently living at or below poverty level: 65.5%

Presented by Edward E. Ford, M.S.W., to the American Educational Research Association at their annual conference on April 20, 1995, in San Francisco.

BRANDT PUBLISHING ORDER FORM

Books	Price	Qty.	Subtotal
DISCIPLINE FOR HOME AND SCHOOL, BOOK ONE	$15.00	___	_____
DISCIPLINE FOR HOME AND SCHOOL, BOOK TWO	$15.00	___	_____
FREEDOM FROM STRESS	$10.00	___	_____
LOVE GUARANTEED	$9.00	___	_____
CHOOSING TO LOVE	$9.00	___	_____
PERMANENT LOVE	$8.00	___	_____
MAKING SENSE OF BEHAVIOR, W. T. Powers	$15.00	___	_____
Videos (add $5.00 for PAL format)			
THE HEART OF THE PROCESS (RTP & PCT)	$15.00	___	_____
TEACHING RESPONSIBLE THINKING	$10.00	___	_____
LOVE GUARANTEED	$10.00	___	_____
PERCEPTUAL CONTROL THEORY, Powers	$15.00	___	_____
Reference Cards			
100 RTP CARDS	$5.00	___	_____

Minimum shipping and handling charge per order $4.50

TOTAL _____

Name (please print) _____

Address _____

_____

_____

Home Phone _____ Business Phone _____

Please note: Prepayment by check only is required on all orders; the only exceptions are purchase orders from school districts. Additional shipping outside the U.S. Book discounts for book stores; no discounts on tapes or cards. Write or call about quantity discounts. All prices subject to change (check current prices at www.brandtpublishing.com).

BRANDT PUBLISHING, 10209 N. 56TH ST.,
SCOTTSDALE, AZ 85253, phone/fax 480-991-4860

Australian Orders: RTP APPLICATIONS, P.O. Box 210,
Coorparoo, Queensland 4151, phone 0417 784 421